What's Next Lord?

By

Timothy L. Grassinger
Pastor

The greatest gift anyone can give is the example of faith.

Order this book online at www.trafford.com
or email orders@trafford.com

Most Trafford titles are also available at major online book retailers.

Print information available on the last page.

ISBN: 978-1-4120-9225-8 (sc)
ISBN: 978-1-4122-0703-4 (e)

Trafford rev. 10/23/2019

North America & international
toll-free: 1 888 232 4444 (USA & Canada)
fax: 812 355 4082

Acknowledgements

I had a lot of help in the preparation of this book. Many thanks are due to Col. Thomas Bowie, USAF retired, my wife Mary and my daughter Lori for the hours spent in editing. Also I have a deep debt of love and gratitude to my wife for her encouragement and patience while I spent many hours on the computer writing and rewriting.

Many thanks are due to the members of the congregations I served over the 40 years of my ministry. They were patient as I grew more proficient in my ministry and accepted my style, frailties and shortcomings. But they always knew that I loved them and I felt their love and supporting prayers in return.

The picture on the cover of this book is of 14,110 feet high Pikes Peak, which was taken from our deck.

Preface

One of the greatest gifts and biggest challenges that God can give is the call into the Holy Ministry. It is the greatest gift because there is no higher calling than to be charged with the care and feeding of God's sheep and bringing the message of the Gospel of salvation to those who are lost. It is the biggest challenge because the responsibility for the welfare of a person's eternal soul knows no equal and with that responsibility comes a life so filled with unusual situations that few can imagine.

The pastoral profession has to be one of the most varied occupations there is, one filled with all kinds of interesting stories. The problem is that many of them cannot be told for reasons of confidentiality. In my book the names are changed or withheld to maintain that confidentiality and to protect the innocent, the guilty and the embarrassed.

I have often cried and many times laughed at where my Lord has led me. It has been a wild ride and yet a pleasurable experience. So I would like to share the joys, laughs, trials and sorrows of a life of service to the Lord. I invite you to hang on for the ride and laugh and cry with me at the situations of life. Along the way we'll identify with human nature at its best, worst and funniest.

Theological students may read this book and gain valuable insight because seminary courses in pastoral theology present examples that are often ivory tower. In these pages I present the real world of the ministry with gusto, humor, pathos, romance and insight.

Chapter 1 – When the Lord Calls, I Listen

"(God) has saved us and called us with his holy calling, not according to our works, but according to his own purpose and grace which he has given us in Christ Jesus..." II Timothy 1:9

"Speak Lord, your servant is listening!" That's what Samuel said to God when He called him the third time. I don't know how many times the Lord called me before I listened. But when He finally cracked the wall of the life I had planned, it was compelling. I was 18 at the time and believed that the whole world lay before me. I had a dream of being a mechanical engineer. Enrolled in the University of Minnesota College of Engineering, I had a sublime vision of receiving a degree, obtaining a lucrative position with a solid company, and investing in a beautiful home in the woods nestled by a lake. Then I would marry the perfect woman and raise children all of whom would be perfectly obedient, well-adjusted, smart and good looking. And we would all live happily ever after.

Well, the Lord had other ideas.

The first time the Lord whispered in my ear was during a physics test that I was taking in an auditorium crammed with 250 engineering students. Half way through I felt like the pressure of the test taking was getting to me and I needed to stretch a little. As I implemented a little Jack La Lanne maneuver with my neck I experienced a vision where the students unexpectedly took the form of computers and a voice came into my head that said, "You want to work with people, not computers." I didn't understand what it meant at the time or even that the Lord was calling me, but it made enough of an impression so that I remembered the incident.

Later that summer, Walt and his wife, Phyllis, relatives of my mother came to visit from Bismarck, North Dakota. Walt was a pastor in the Reformed Church and he seemed to thrive in his ministry. He was an impressive man with strong features and a compassionate countenance. His bearing was of a gifted and caring pastor.

As we ate lunch, he drew me into conversation about my life and activities in the church. I told him about my studying engineering in college, but that I was not sure I wanted to continue in that field. I also shared with him that I was active in my church ushering, singing in the choir, teaching Sunday school and working with our youth group.

Then he said it! "Tim, have you ever thought about becoming a pastor?"

He could have hit me over the head with a baseball bat and I couldn't have been more stunned. No! I had not thought about becoming a pastor. But I wondered, why not? I had always been active in my church from the time I was knee high. It's possible that I avoided the idea because I didn't think I could live up to the dignity of the pastoral office. My pastor, Carl Bolle, stood six foot three inches tall and had to be closer to God than my five foot six. He was dignified and proper. I was young and fun loving. The thought of being dignified like you would expect a pastor to be—especially like my pastor—was nowhere to be found in the recesses of my mind. I couldn't be like that. Maybe my mind was too clogged with the idea of the success of being an engineer. Maybe full time work in the church was just too close to me that I hadn't considered it.

But now I started to.

The third leg of my call from the Lord was on a summer evening in the courtyard of our church. I was visiting with some friends when out of the blue a high school classmate said, "Tim, how would you like to take an entrance exam to Concordia College?" Concordia was a college to prepare men and women for the teaching or preaching ministry of our church. My mouth dropped open and I asked him, "Why?" And he said, "Because I think you would make a good minister." Well, you don't have to hit me too many times with an idea before I get the drift and I said, "Speak Lord, your servant is listening." I took the entrance exam.

In the fall I entered Concordia College as a student preparing for the ministry. As I walked the beautiful, serene campus with the 20-foot tall statue of Martin Luther holding an open Bible in his hand and met the friendly, dedicated students all who wanted to serve their Lord in some special way, I said to myself, "This is where the Lord wants me." Now my life seemed to stretch before me so naturally. I was comfortable that I was following the lead of my loving Lord who had given so much to me and required so little in return.

Since that time the Lord has led me on an incredible journey, one filled with testing and sustaining, stress and blessing, sadness and humor. However, I always was comforted by my faith that God was with me every step of the way. Come along and share my journey!

Chapter 2 – Finding a Wonderful Wife

" He who finds a wife finds what is good and receives favor from God." Proverbs 18:22

Do we really ever *find* anything? Most of our life we are in the "lose it" mode which is followed by the "search" mode and if God wills it, maybe, just maybe we find it. So, when I speak of "finding" a wonderful wife, I mean that, most certainly. Lemuel in Proverbs 31 says: "If you can find a truly good wife, she is worth more than precious gems! Her husband can trust her, and she will satisfy his needs. She will not hinder him, but help him all her life. (Proverbs 31:10-12 The Living Bible)

God led me to her.

He knew that she would be a blessing for me, and also a wonderful helpmate in my ministry. She would keep me on the straight path and guide me when I needed it, which was not rare. She was hobbling on a broken ankle and interested in someone else for most of my first year at Concordia College so I didn't pay much attention and don't remember even seeing her on campus. But following her break up with Ted, the Lord brought us together in two classes for the last quarter of the school year.

There was to be a test in one of these classes called Physical Science. This particular test was on geology and the identification of rocks. On the evening before the test I went to the room where all of the rocks were neatly laid out with their labels. I had about an hour head start in memorizing the identity of the rocks before Mary arrived. I hadn't expected to see her that night, but when she entered the room, I couldn't take my eyes off of her. I thought she was the most beautiful girl I had seen at Concordia. I wondered *why hadn't I taken notice of her before?* She had short, light brown hair with eyes that melted my heart and could not be obscured even by the cat eye frames of her glasses. Her cheeks were rosy from being out in the chilling winds of the Minnesota winter. She smiled at me as she walked past and I just could not resist trying to impress her by rattling off the names of all the rocks.

I thought that must have caught her attention. But instead of impressing her, she told me later that she thought I was an arrogant showoff. Oblivious to her feelings and thinking that I was on good ground with her, I blundered on.

The next morning I came to school early to review the rocks again before the test. Mary was there once more, still struggling to relate the rocks with their names. Our eyes met and I smiled at her and she gave me a look that told me she needed to concentrate on rocks.

On another occasion, I tried to help her with the understanding of a table of facts from our economics class and gave her a long involved explanation that she could see right away was bogus. My next bungle was right on the heels of the last. We shared a class on the life of St. Paul the apostle and we were to have a test on his missionary journeys. The professor was aware that several files of his tests and notes were floating around the student body. He encouraged the students to get a hold of a file and study from it. He didn't view it as cheating, but a way to focus the student's studying. A friend of mine located one of those files, studied from it and passed it on to me. There wasn't much time left before the test, so I studied it quickly and then tried to give Mary a few tips on what was in it. The professor told us we would be required to draw a map of one of Paul's missionary journeys that he would select. I carefully calculated from the dated tests in the file that if the professor were going in a rotation, he would ask us to draw a map of the third missionary journey. But when the test was handed out, wouldn't you know, he wanted us to draw Paul's second journey. I couldn't even look at Mary after the test was over. I knew that I had made one of the biggest errors of my life. Not only would our grades suffer but also I believed that she had lost all confidence in me.

However, the Lord decided that we were to be together even though I didn't know it yet. Maybe it was a combination that Mary was from North Dakota, where my mother was born, and that she had broken up with her steady and that she liked to scuff my meticulously polished shoes, but I was determined not to give up.

On the slim chance that I might see her again, on a whim, I drove to the Concordia campus on Sunday afternoon.

Wow! The Lord was shining on me. There was Mary with some of her friends. I pulled over in my polished, two tone blue 1956 Chevy and asked the girls if they would like a ride. At first there was a mixed reaction, a quick huddle and suddenly a consensus that they would accept the ride. I was pleased when somehow the seating arrangement worked out so that Mary sat beside me. The ride turned out to be only three blocks to Walgreen's. I couldn't believe how any ride that I wanted to last forever could go so fast. It seemed like I just stepped on the gas and I was already applying the brakes at the drug store. The girls went inside and I waited in the car. I could have gone in with Mary and tried to make more points with her, but the girls said they would be gone only a few minutes, so I waited. That was probably better for my "point getting" anyway.

The minutes dragged on slowly. After what seemed forever, but was probably only 15 minutes, I was sure that they had slipped out the back door to allude me.

Before long, they returned laughing and talking excitedly. I was so vain as to hope they were talking about me.

When they got closer, I could hear that they weren't.

Divine providence or plan, I don't know which, once more seated Mary beside me as we drove to the campus. In a flash we were back too soon.

Now was my chance to ask her for a date, but I was too embarrassed to do it in front of all the girls. I thought how terrible I'd feel if she turned me down with them looking on. I felt the opportunity slipping away until the girls began to walk away and I called Mary back. "Would you care to go on a drive to Como Park?" I blurted out. "Sure, that sounds nice," she answered. Now I was in heaven! She chose to be with me. We drove to the Como Park Conservatory where there were generous varieties of exotic and local plants and flowers. Again, I tried to put on the impressing mode, as I bragged that I could identify the names of the plants and flowers because I worked for a florist. She tested me a couple of times and I came through with the names with flying colors, which seemed to impress her. I think she chose to ignore the fact the all of the plants and flowers were labeled.

After our stroll through the conservatory, I was warm all over. I thought it was my growing emotions for Mary getting the best of me, but it was only the heat of the green house. Things were going so well that I decided to press on. As we drove back to the campus, I asked if she would like to go to a movie that evening. She answered that she really shouldn't, as she had to work on a paper that was due the next day. I have never pleaded with a girl to go out with me before, but I did this time. She finally agreed to the date but said, "I'll have to take a late grade on the paper, but all right."

Now my heart began to pound with such excitement that I thought it might jump out of my chest. The macho in me tried to conceal my emotions but my heart sang as I drove home to get ready for our date.

After checking the drive-in movie schedule, I picked her up at the dorm and asked her if she had seen the movie, "North by Northwest?" She said she hadn't. So off we went. At the movie she was happy that I bought her food. Pop and popcorn was all I could afford. Halfway into the movie, as the fugitives climbed over the president's faces carved into Mount Rushmore, she remembered that she had seen the movie before. She kept that her little secret until much later in our relationship.

The dorm rules were that Mary had to be back by midnight, so we had to leave the movie early. I apologized to her for not being able to see the end, but she never let on that she already knew how it ended.

One thing I learned already on that first date, I didn't want our relationship to ever end.

We enjoyed one more date before Mary went home for the summer. It was one of the most wonderful times of my life as we drove to St. Croix Falls, which is on the border between Minnesota and Wisconsin. The spring day was warm and the scenery was beautiful as our conversation flowed easily. I learned so much about this wonderful woman. She was intelligent, compassionate and down to earth. I was impressed and the more I got to know her, the more I knew she was the one I wanted to share my life with.

At the time, I didn't understand all that would involve.

We did see each other briefly during the summer. Mary attended a friend's wedding in Trimont, Minnesota, and she wrote to me that she could arrange a 24-hour layover in the Twin Cities on her return trip. We arranged that I would drive to the Greyhound Bus depot in Minneapolis to pick her up. But I miscalculated the time it would take to get there and I arrived a few minutes after the bus pulled in. As I rushed into the depot my heart pounded with the thought that she would be upset that I wasn't there to greet her when she arrived. I spotted Mary pulling her suitcase toward the front door. Our eyes met and I could see a relieved expression on her face. It was wonderful to see her again. She was as beautiful as I remembered.

We kissed.

Then she told me that when she got off the bus a matronly lady asked her if her name was Mary. As she answered, "Yes," she thought to herself, *Oh that Tim! He must have sent his mother to pick me up.* As she followed the woman towing her suitcase behind her, she was waiting for an introduction. But the lady just talked about all the housework she had for her to do. It didn't take but a moment for Mary to decide this wasn't my mother and that she wasn't going home with her to do any housework! They parted company with the lady frantically looking for another Mary to do her housecleaning.

We drove home. My mother was eagerly awaiting the opportunity to meet Mary and she was sitting at her desk when we came in the front door. I can still see the look on her face as she saw

Mary for the first time and it spoke volumes. Her expressive smile communicated her thoughts that told me *this is the best one of all of the girls you have brought home. She could be the one I have in mind for you.*

But I already knew that.

Most of our romance, during the time of Mary's college preparations to be a parochial school teacher, was by mail. She went on to Concordia College in River Forest, Illinois in a suburb of Chicago. I went to Concordia Seminary in Springfield, which is about 200 miles south of Chicago. We did see each other occasionally.

There was the time right after Christmas when I drove to Bismarck, North Dakota to exchange Christmas gifts. My underlying purpose was to give Mary a diamond ring and ask her to marry me. I planned to pop the question the same night that I arrived, but Mary's mother experienced the symptoms of a heart attack and was taken to the hospital. That foiled my plan.

Now, what do I do?

Do I go ahead and propose? Do I give Mary the ring and take the risk of her mother dieing from the shock? That would really endear me to the family and forever leave a blotch on my record!

I decided to wait.

Now I really felt cheap as we exchanged gifts and she gave me some very nice things and I was only equipped with a few token gifts like a pair of fir-lined gloves and a monogrammed hanky. The ring was burning a hole in my pocket, but I didn't dare give it to her.

Thanks be to God, Mary's mother recovered.

As we traveled back to college, I hatched a new plan to give her the ring at the stroke of midnight on New Year's Eve. Our plans were to be with my roommate, Al and his date for the New Year's Eve communion worship at his church and then go to a party at his home. It was there that I would propose at the stroke of midnight at the ringing in of the New Year. How romantic!

At church, when we went to the railing for communion, I must have been super sensitive because I thought the ring fell out of my suit pocket. That was physically impossible, but I didn't want to pre-empt the appointed time by dropping the ring on the floor. I pictured myself having to drop to my knees and searching for the ring like a dog looking for its bone. So I kept my arm in a hooked position to make sure that the ring wouldn't get loose. Mary gave me a couple of funny looks wondering why my arm was in such a strange position. But she never asked the question.

Finally the opportunity came for me to check on the ring's location and I was relieved to find that it was safely tucked away in my inside coat pocket where it belonged.

When we arrived at Al's, the stage was set that just before midnight everyone would gradually leave the room so that Mary wouldn't get suspicious. We would be left alone so that I could "pop the question." The appointed hour finally arrived and we were alone. I got down on one knee and reached into my pocket. I repeated the magic words, "Mary, I love you and want to spend the rest of my life with you. Will you marry me?" I opened the box to display an emerald cut diamond in a plain setting. Mary's response was not what I expected and I am still astounded by what came out of her mouth.

She looked at the ring with her eyes opened wide and asked, "Is it real?" For some reason, she thought that I was playing a practical joke on her and the ring came from a box of Cracker Jacks.

Yes, it's real! Now will you answer my question?"

"What question?"

"Will you marry me?" By now I was a little perturbed and my voice gave me away.

Finally the answer that I wanted came. Mary, in a rather matter-of-fact voice said, "Yes, of course I'll marry you!"

We were married the next year on December 29th, 1962 in snowy and cold Bismarck. But our marriage has never grown cold over all the years we have been married. The Lord blessed us with three children, of which we are very proud. Now we have four beautiful and entertaining grandchildren.

This was the start of something wonderful. We have gone through many joys and trials of life and ministry together. Mary has always been by my side to give me love and support and to be my strength. She has served in her own ministry in the church by teaching children, actively participating in church life, and being an excellent example of a Christian wife and mother who dedicates her life to her Lord and to serving her family. She has blessed my life and ministry by her loving support in many ways.

But most of all she has been my gift from God. Mary has been as Lemuel said, "a truly good wife, worth more than precious gems!"

Chapter 3 – Worship Practices in Otter Creek

"Come, let us bow down in worship, let us kneel before the Lord our Maker; for he is our God and we are the people of his pasture, the flock under his care." Psalm 95:6-7

A minister who loses his sense of humor is in deep trouble. I have often said, "God has a sense of humor—He made us didn't he?"

One of the lighter times of my ministry was while on vicarage (internship) in the summer of 1961, in North Dakota. I was serving a little congregation of 55 people in a rural Russian-German settlement on the plains called Otter Creek. The church was a typical small white frame building sitting on the top of a hill with a one-room schoolhouse next door and the obligatory cemetery behind. A steep flight of steps led up to the front double doors and a steeple with a bell tower cast shadows from the morning sun.

I was to begin serving the church on Sunday morning and had driven to Bismarck a couple of days before and was staying at the home of Mary and her parents. Very early Sunday morning Mary and I drove the 60 miles west to St. Paul's Lutheran Church at Otter Creek for the purpose of conducting a service at 9:00 a.m. We found the church, arriving a little early, which was just fine because it gave me a chance to get acquainted with the layout. But the hour of 9 O'clock came and went and no one showed up for the service. Now this knocked the wind out of the sails of this new student minister who was trying to maintain his courage. I started to wonder if some word of my ability preceded me to Otter Creek and everyone decided to stay home.

Finally it dawned on us that we had crossed the time zone, which ran in conjunction with the Missouri River and split Bismarck from Mandan. We were an hour early! Whew, what a relief! After another half hour we could see some dust rising from the gravel road to the south of the church. When the car arrived at the church it contained the chairman of the trustees whose job it was to dust the pews before everyone arrived. The whole family came with him freshly scrubbed and dressed in their Sunday finest. The father wore dark blue dress pants with a white shirt, bolo tie and cowboy boots. The mother wore a proper print dress and the two boys, about 11 and 12, wore freshly pressed jeans with cowboy shirts and boots.

The daughter was 6 and she had on a miniature dress that matched her mother's. It was evident that mother made them both. The three men wore cowboy hats which they removed respectfully as they entered the church. It was obvious that they were a little shy at meeting their new summer vicar. The children giggled as the parents greeted us politely and quietly went about their business of dusting the pews. Each member of the family did their part.

While they were going about their business, I tried to get some moisture in my nervous, dry mouth so that I could preach.

At last the people started to arrive and all were very cordial. Mary and I greeted each one and then it was time for me to get my preaching robe on. Mary sat down in the pew and the Lord guided her to just the right place. You see, the custom in that church was that all the men sat on one side and all the women sat on the other. Also, there was age discrimination. The children sat up front and as you got older you could move toward the back. Either Mary picked just the right place or everyone adjusted his or her seating to accommodate her. If it was a matter of accommodation, the members continued that practice the rest of the summer. That's just the way they operated. They were people of few words, respectful and very obliging.

After being at St. Paul's about a month, I wondered why the two candles sitting proudly on the altar were never lighted. At first I thought it was because these Russian-German farmers were frugal and that the candles were there for decoration. Then I considered that they were only to be lighted for Holy Communion. A few weeks later came a Sunday on which we were going to celebrate communion, but the candles still had not been lighted. Now, I really wondered if they were only for decoration. But as I got into the worship service, I forgot about the candles until after the sermon and I handed the offering plates to the ushers. Because the church was so small, it didn't make much sense to sit down while the offering was received, so I stood at the altar with my back to the congregation. Immediately I felt the church start to shake with the footsteps of someone coming down the aisle. I knew it was too soon for the ushers to be bringing the offering forward so, out of curiosity I cast a glance over my shoulder to see what was happening. What I saw caused a shiver of fear to run down my back. It was the chairman of the elders striding down the aisle toward me. I can still remember the sight vividly in my mind. He was wearing brown western pants, a white western shirt, broad red suspenders and cowboy boots. The look on his face was as stern and resolute as I had ever seen him and I interpreted it as anger. I was thankful he was not wearing spurs.

My mind went berserk.

All I could think of was that I had said something offensive in my sermon and he was coming to throw me out. But I couldn't figure out what I might have said. It took only three seconds for him to travel the distance down that short aisle before he was standing directly behind me and I could feel his hot breath on my neck. Everything became embarrassingly silent. I wished a distracting sound would divert people's attention so I could vanish, but it didn't happen. Even the old pump organ that his wife played during the offering was silent.

My heart pounded with fear as I looked over my shoulder expecting to see the elder reach for the back of my neck and the seat of my pants to throw me out the door. But instead, what I saw surprised me. He was reaching deep into his pants pocket and searching with an exaggerated motion. Finally he came up with a "farmer" match, which you can strike on almost anything.

What followed is etched permanently in my mind.

He looked down and tipped his foot to expose the sole of his boot. I could almost read his mind as the portly elder thought, *if I strike the match on my shoe I might fall over and embarrass myself.* Next he looked at the altar wondering where he could strike the match there. By the expression on his face it was obvious that he was thinking, *that would be sacrilegious.*

I couldn't believe what he did next.

He reached down, folded back the material covering the zipper of his fly, struck that match on it and proceeded to light those two communion candles. Then he strode back to his place and sat down with a satisfied look of accomplishing a job well done.

I was grateful that I was facing the altar and didn't have to look at the congregation for I would have cracked up in laughter.

With a deep sense of relief, I received the offering from the ushers, fumbled through the distribution of the Lord's Supper and concluded the service with the benediction. All the while my mind was reflecting on my seminary course on liturgics and I couldn't wait to get back to class and tell the students how they light the candles at St. Paul's Lutheran Church at Otter Creek.

Later, I got wind of a story that was going around the congregation before my arrival. It had nothing to do with my ministry capability or lack-there-of. The word came from the district president that the church at Otter Creek was getting a summer vicar and the neighboring church in Hannover was getting a pastor from the same seminary. The individual who was passing the news said, if he were remembering correctly, "The vicar was tall and the pastor was short." When I arrived on the scene first and stood a full 5 foot 6 inches tall, the members wondered just how short the pastor would be!

I learned some important lessons at Otter Creek. Be ready for anything, don't anticipate that you are the problem and let things play out. Until you are sure of what the situation is about don't blow it out of proportion.

Pastor Tim in the pulpit at St. Paul's Lutheran Church Otter Creek, North Dakota

Chapter 4 – More Memories of Otter Creek

"...let the fields be jubilant, and everything in them." Psalm 96:12

The people of St. Paul's Lutheran Church were warm and friendly. It was a good place to try my first wings at ministry. I learned a lot about human nature and how differently people will react to situations. Observing people can be a wonderful learning experience and be very helpful in dealing with them in a way that meets their spiritual and social needs, for the two are usually intertwined.

Remember that these people were of Russian-German descent, so they were quite conservative. They wasted nothing. Even their words were carefully metered so as not to waste a one. They loved socializing with one another and most of them were related in some way. Families had homesteaded in the area, worked the fields and they stayed for generations. This was their land and livelihood. Their church linked them to the Lord who gave them strength and it was also the center of their social life. They worked very hard from sun-up to sunset in the fields or in their barns.

I lived with the Tony Vetter family that summer--the father, Tony, his wife, Alice, and a 13 year-old son, Alvin. They arose before dawn every morning and were milking 18 cows before breakfast. After a few mornings of sleeping until they came in for breakfast, I began to feel guilty, so this city kid climbed out of bed and helped milk cows. They let me milk old Anna who gave so plentifully that she squirted her milk as she entered the barn.

After breakfast, into the fields Tony and Alvin would go. Alice would stay behind to clean up the morning dishes and prepare a midmorning lunch and start dinner. I usually busied myself with church work, making calls, studying, or preparing for the Sunday service. Sometimes I was free to help them in the fields.

This particular day was one of those times and I was excited. The family was to begin stacking bundles of wheat stalks into piles and I was invited to help. They even thought to invite Mary to come from Bismarck to spend the day. Wow, That was going to be great!

I called Mary the night before to make plans. The telephone system in the country was a party line system that left much to be desired as far as privacy was concerned. In fact, "listening in" was the accepted way of finding out what was going on in the area. No one thought of it as being nosey, it was a way of life – a sort of local

CNN or Fox News. So when I called Mary, the signal began fairly strong. But as our conversation went on and more receivers were picked up on the line, the weaker the signal became until at the end of our conversation I had to yell into the phone, "Honey, I love you!" I heard a half a dozen giggles over the phone and I hung up a little embarrassed.

The plan, which seemed like a good one, was to have Mary ride out from Bismarck early in the morning to the nearby town of Hannover with Mr. and Mrs. Bornham, who ran a small store there. First thing in the morning I would take the pickup truck and drop the milk off at the dairy, get my sermon approved by my "tall" supervising pastor, and pick up some rolls of binder twine that Tony needed from the Bornham store.

I was up at the crack of dawn and everything was going like clock work until I got to the dairy. It wasn't open yet, so I decided to go to the parsonage with my sermon. Never thinking that it was before 6 A.M., I was surprised that I awoke Pastor Sharenburg, who came to the door in his pajamas. Without opening the door he asked what I wanted so early in the morning so I waved my sermon copy in front of the window. With blurry eyes he dismissed me briskly saying, "I trust your sermons are acceptable by now Tim, so just go and preach it. And you don't have to get them approved anymore especially before six in the morning!" Without another word he disappeared into the recesses of his parsonage.

By now the dairy was open for business so I dropped off the milk. Then I hurried over to Bornham's store where I had to wait until they arrived. There was Mary in the back seat of the car looking so good. Excitedly Mary and I hopped into the pickup and headed back to the farm. Upon our arrival the whole family came out to greet her and made her feel welcome. But Tony looked into the back of the truck and asked, "Where's the binder twine?" In all the excitement of having Mary there, I forgot the twine. I could tell that Tony was not too happy, but he didn't say a word. He just got into the truck and drove back to Hannover to get it. But just to be sure I got the message he pealed out as he left. Tony considered burning rubber wasteful and he would never do such a thing unless he was a little peeved.

We were delayed from getting into the field by my absent mindedness, but the sun was bright and warm and I was learning something new called shocking. What was important was that Mary was with me. All was well for me at Otter Creek. Tony showed me how to take two bundles and set them firmly against each other in the stubble of the field. He explained that this was most important to do right so that the other bundles that were placed around the first two would stay in place. Four bundles were placed around the first two and a seventh was placed on top of the stack to protect the grain. The process seemed easy enough.

Tony and I started out evenly in our respective rows. I noticed how easy and fluid his movements were. He didn't waste a move. With a rhythmic motion he placed the two bundles together and proceeded to build his shocks one after the other. It was difficult for me to get into the rhythm, but I felt that I could keep up with him by working a little faster. I believed that I had youth on my side and that would compensate for inexperience.

Wrong!

No matter how hard or fast I worked, Tony was gradually pulling away from me. I would shove the two bundles together and while I was reaching for a third, the first two would fall over. Then I would have to start all over while Tony's shocks stood tall and strong and never fell. Alvin and his mother were having their own competition a few rows away. Mary tried to help me for a while but she had dressed in black in order to look good for me. The heat of the bright sun caused her to get too warm and she started to get dizzy. She spent most of the rest of the day in the shade of the truck assuming the duty of occasionally bringing us water.

By morning lunch break Tony was noticeably ahead of me. By noon it was obviously no contest. And by late afternoon he was so far ahead that he had disappeared over the next hill and I was so exhausted that I could barely move.

Tony finished his row and started working back toward me on mine. When we finally met, the sun was getting low in the horizon. Tony seemed to have the same strength that he started with that morning. I, on the other hand, was sweaty, so dirty that I looked as though I had been rolling in the dirt and totally exhausted. He smiled at me and said, "Ready to call it a day?" I could only nod my head.

Alice left the field early to prepare supper. While Mary and I cleaned up, Tony and Alvin did the milking and then came into the house for one of my favorite meals. Alice had prepared a German specialty called fleish kuchla. It was a main dish of a tablespoon of hamburger and one of sausage, onions, salt and pepper sealed in a pocket of dough and deep fat fried until golden brown. She would serve the fleish kuchla hot off the stove and when bitten into, the juices would run down my chin. It was soooo good! Today I know that fleish kuchla was great for clogging arteries. But we were young then and who cared.

After supper our tummies were full and we were tired but happy. I drove Mary home, which because of the time zone, took two hours to get to Bismarck and no time to get home.

The next day was Saturday and in the evening I decided that I should go over to the church and practice that sermon that Pastor Sharenburg had declared acceptable without looking at it.

The church was about a 3-mile drive up a curvy dirt road. It sat on the top of a solitary hill and from its vantage point there were no signs of life. By the time I arrived at the church the last glimpse of daylight had disappeared. The church was always unlocked. Who would disturb it way out there in the middle of nowhere? I climbed into the pulpit and began the oratorio of my sermon. I completed it once and started through it the second time. The wind began to blow whistling against the church and it started to creak. The windows rattled and I could hear the wooden shingles being lifted up by the strength of the wind. An involuntary shiver went through my body. But I shook it off.

Come on! You are a grown man and a seminary student. You have no reason to fear. There is no one around. --- That's just the point! As I continued with my sermon the wind blew harder and it seemed like the church was beginning to lean a little. I tried to put all of my concentration into the practicing of my message, but my mind kept picturing the cemetery out back. I imagined seeing things blowing out there and things being disturbed in the shadows and---. *Oh come on now! There is no such thing as ghosts or spirits from the dead!*

Briefly the wind let up and. I was sure that I heard voices and someone walking outside.

A gust of wind blew again and this time the church doors were rattling like someone was trying to get in. *You know, I can practice this sermon just as well back at the farm.* I gathered up my papers and headed for the door. *Should I go out there? Come on Tim! The Lord is with you. There is nothing to fear! I know that but I would feel much safer in my room!*

I ran for the car, jumped in, locked the doors and drove back to the farmhouse as fast as I could. Dirt flew as I sped around the curves. The blowing weeds from the sides of the road seemed to be reaching out for me as I zipped by.

When I got home, I took three deep breaths and threw my shoulders back and walked into the house as if nothing were wrong. "Getting windy out there," I said to Tony who was reading the newspaper. "Yup!" he said, "Going to stir up something no good, I recon."

Sunday after church, Tony suggested that we drive out to the field and check the shocks we had worked on so hard. I always wondered if he suspected that, when we got there, we would find his shocks all standing and at least half of mine lying on the ground. And so it was. Was it my ineptness at shocking or was it those ghosts stirring up "something no good?"

The Lord taught me that day that it is good to try something new and different, but when push comes to shove, a pastor better stick to the things he knows best—the preaching of God's Word. But I learned how to speak the language of farming and that was a great help in my first parish in rural South Dakota.

Author's note: St. Paul's Lutheran Church closed its doors later that year marking the end of an era. The members had to make the choice whether to worship at the church in New Salem or Hannover. Today St. Paul's Lutheran Church, together with the school, proudly stands on a service road along Interstate Highway 94, at New Salem, N.D. about 37 miles west of Bismarck. It was moved there as a testimony to its historical significance—a living tribute to the strength of the people who settled in the prairies of North Dakota. They left the cemetery where it was.

Pastor Tim and Mary in front of St. Paul's Church

Chapter 5 - The Day of Ups and Downs

"Do not boast about tomorrow, for you do not know what each day may bring." Proverbs 27:1

Everyone has a day they can look back on and say, "Lord, that was quite a day and I am glad that you were with me!" It was in the spring of 1969. I had completed my seminary training and was serving three churches in South Dakota. Two of the churches I was called to and the third I was serving as a vacancy.

The telephone woke me from a sound sleep early that morning. It was a member of Peace Lutheran Church, which was 20 miles north from where we lived in Columbia. Peace was one of the churches I was called to serve. The member reported, "There was a terrible accident directly in front of our church. Two families from the church were involved in a head on collision and three people were dead!"

I slugged down some breakfast and headed north. When I arrived my mind tried to make sense out of the meager facts I knew, but I couldn't. I felt like a detective as I visited with the highway patrol, family survivors and members of the church. As I pieced information together a rather chilling story emerged. I had no idea that the two couples involved were known as "snoops," who went around poking their nose in other people's business. The couples had agreed that they would go snooping that evening. At the last minute the wife of one of the snoops decided she didn't feel well and chose to stay home. That decision saved her life and allowed her to continue raising her young children.

During the night some disagreement must have come between these "snoops". Witnesses observed them driving very fast past each other on the highway in front of the church. They were playing "chicken" driving toward each other at great speeds to see who would "chicken out" and be the first to steer away from a collision course.

The next thing anyone heard was a loud crash, and then silence.

The first to happen on the scene were two teenagers from our church who were returning from a date. They saw an unusual light shining in one of the ditches along the road and they stopped to investigate. One car was at the bottom of the ditch with a door flung open. The grotesque sight of two dead bodies, they recognized were eerily illuminated by the car's dome light. The teenagers were very shaken by what they saw.

The gossip going around the community was that the lady who died in the car with her husband was pregnant by the man in the other car. From the information I had gathered, I concluded that the game of chicken was a result of the infidelity coming to light and anger raging between the husbands. Autopsies were never performed nor was a pregnancy test ever done, so this remains speculation.

I ministered to the surviving wife who was pretty shook-up but very thankful that the Lord guided her so that she had not gone along and was alive to raise her three youngsters. There was no family of the deceased couple in the area to minister to. The teenagers who came upon the accident were in school so I didn't want to bother them at that time. I would talk to them at the youth meeting on Sunday. Their parents assured me that their teens were dealing with their emotions very well and visiting with them on Sunday would be soon enough. Somewhat exhausted, I headed for home.

Mary had prepared one of my favorite casseroles out of love and consideration for what I had just been through. Before I had a chance to take a bite the doorbell rang. It was a member of our local church in Columbia who was in panic. Tears were streaming down her face. She rattled off with great emotion that her daughter and son-in-law had taken her three-year-old granddaughter to the hospital in Aberdeen. The diagnosis was not good. It was spinal meningitis! This struck fear into our hearts as it brought to mind a beautiful three-year-old girl from our church who had died from that disease only a few months earlier.

I jammed a couple of bites of that delicious casserole into my mouth and headed for my car. During the entire 20-minute drive to the hospital in Aberdeen, I bargained with God in prayer like Abraham did for Sodom and Gomorrah. I had never prayed so hard before.

"Lord, this couple is just starting out in their life together blessed by the gift of their little daughter. They are coming to church but they need reassurance for their faith rather than trial. Please, do not take away their precious little daughter from them. Do not give them reason to turn from you, but rather reveal your powerful grace and love by healing their child from this sickness."

Upon arriving at the hospital I headed for the little girl's room. The parents were huddled together at a round table in the dimly lit hallway. Fear racked their young faces and they were clenching each other's hands.

They were just kids.

They were married at 19 and this was their first child. The young mother was pretty with blond hair and a china doll complexion. She was dressed like she should be in high school. The father had a rugged handsomeness about him with a tan face from working in the fields. His short, brown hair revealed the white circle marking the tan line where his cap blotted out the sun. He hadn't taken the time to change his clothes from the field.

At the same moment that I sat down to join them, the doctor came out of the room where their daughter lay. He looked at the couple as he walked by shrugging his shoulders as if to say, "There isn't much hope." His face showed so much grief for this child and her parents that he couldn't say a word to them. He disappeared down the hall.

The couple filled me in on their desperate situation. Their daughter woke up with a high fever and everything that the mother tried to bring it down failed. She called the doctor and he told her to bring the child directly to the hospital. There in the hospital corridor at the table we prayed together for the child. A nurse came out of the room and told us we could go in.

There was the incredible sight of the tiny three-year-old lying face up on the full size hospital bed. She looked so small and pale as she lay there unconscious. I tried to be comforting to the couple, but soon words failed and I thought the best thing we could do was pray.

We prayed together for God to touch this little girl with His healing power.

"Loving Lord," I prayed. "Look upon this little child with your great mercy. Wrap her in your gracious and loving arms and have mercy upon her and her parents. Let healing flow into her limp body. Permit her to view again the sun light of your precious days and allow her to grow up to be your child in every way. Grant her a return to full health so that she may serve you all the days of her life. You love the little children, Lord, and desire that they come to you. Do not turn this little one away from the opportunity to give you continued praise and of being your special child in this life. We commend her to your great mercy and implore you to heal her. Lord, hear and answer our prayer in your Son's name. Amen."

As we prayed I noticed that the girl's body shivered involuntarily.

I didn't know how to interpret this movement. I wondered if she was convulsing or if it was a sign of life returning. We visited some more, all the while gazing at this beautiful child of God who appeared to be sound asleep.

It was not long before words failed me again, so I prayed similarly to my first prayer. As I prayed, the little girl's eyes opened. She didn't appear to focus on anything or recognize her parents or surroundings. I wanted to hope that this was a good sign, but I feared it might be an involuntary reflex before death came over her. We continued to talk together of God's love, compassion, and ability to provide miracles even when the science of medicine has reached its limit. I felt that God was compelling me to pray again.

We folded our hands and prayed again asking the Lord to heal this child. This time there appeared to be a marked improvement in the girl. For, as we prayed she blinked her eyes and showed signs of recognition. When we came to the end of the prayer and concluded with "Amen," the girl's grandparents appeared at the door carrying the little girl's favorite stuffed teddy bear.

She immediately sat up, gave a little smile and spoke one word. "Teddy!"

We all heaved a sigh of relief as the realization overwhelmed us that she was going to be all right. Tears of joy filled the eyes of the young mother and the father and grandparents choked back tears. I had a big lump in my throat.

Something very special happened in that hospital room. That little girl's loving Lord and great Good Shepherd had answered our prayers in a miraculous way and gave back her life. He healed her from a very serious illness that could have claimed her for heaven.

I have no doubt that this was God's miraculous answer to our prayers. I firmly believe that out of love and consideration for this young couple's frail faith, our Lord spared the life of this little girl so that she could be the "little child who would lead them" to a deeper faith.

We rejoiced and praised God together with the couple, the grandparents and an astonished doctor and nurses.

Then it was time to go to St. John's Lutheran Church in Groton, my vacancy church, to teach the 7th and 8th grade confirmation class. I had some emotional stories to share with them, one of sadness and one of joy. We all learned an important lesson about the power of God and the efficacy of prayer.

After teaching the class it was 6 P.M. and I drove home thinking that I should be exhausted. But I wasn't tired at all. I was pumped up. My mind was filled with a multitude of thoughts about God and His greatness and how, sometimes, we miss the truth that He can take the worst situations and turn them into good. He is truly a gracious God.

Chapter 6 - Death in the Barn

"O death, where is your sting? The sting of death is sin, and the power of sin is the law. But thanks be to God! He gives us the victory through our Lord Jesus Christ." I Corinthians 15:55-56

Sometimes pastors get involved in situations that seem more like a mystery novel rather than real life.

It was summer now and I was still serving the same three churches. The telephone rang around 10:30 P.M. on a Saturday night. A male voice introduced himself as Bill and said, "I have a lady here who needs your help. Her husband was found dead in a barn and she needs some spiritual help. I'll bring her right up."

Now when getting ready for bed, that kind of news wakes one up quickly. Counseling late on Saturday night is not something a pastor looks forward to when he has to get up early and preach in three churches the next morning, but this was a most important situation. The man who called arrived with the young woman about 30 minutes later. The woman looked to be about 35, of average appearance and was dressed in a well-worn housedress. She was obviously pregnant and the tattered condition of her dress demonstrated that she was not of means. Visibly shaken, her eyes were filled with shock and fear. But, I noticed no tears. The man was not dressed in farming attire, but wore dark slacks with an open collar shirt and a jacket. He appeared to be deliberate and calm and was obviously concerned for the young woman he brought to my office. I was trying to figure out the relationship between these two, but it was not immediately obvious.

He told most of the bizarre account of what had happened that evening. The new widow added a few details. She and her husband were taking care of a farm near Groton, while the owners were on vacation. That evening the husband went to the barn to do the chores while his wife went inside to check on the house. Because she was six months pregnant, the plan was that she would stay in the cool comfort of the house while her husband finished outside.

She lay down on the couch and fell asleep.

When she awoke she was surprised that it was dark and later than she expected. She feared something might have happened to her husband because he hadn't returned from the chores to wake her. I thought it strange that, rather than looking for him alone, she called her friend and they searched for him together.

What they found was the grisly sight of her husband hanging by a rope from a rafter in the barn. They described the scene saying that there was an old milk stool that was lying on its side about 10 feet away from the body. They suggested that he must have kicked it out from under himself.

With great care and patience I counseled the widow into the early hours of the morning reassuring her of God's love and comfort.

When the couple left, the woman was considerably more composed, but she still trembled. I continued to think it strange that she called her friend before she went to look for her husband. I thought that she must have expected something tragic.

With no one around to witness the death, it was considered suicide by the local police and never investigated further. However, bits and pieces of the story began to come out.

The mother of the deceased was a formidable figure. Standing a good 5 foot 10 inches tall with biceps like a weight lifter, she was stronger than many men and could out work the hardiest of them. The day before her son's funeral, she took me aside and filled me in from her perspective. She believed that her son's wife was in a torrid love affair with the "friend" who brought her to the parsonage. She was positive that the baby her daughter-in-law was carrying was not her son's, but rather the boy friend's. She was convinced that they murdered him in order to get him out of the way and so the wife could collect his insurance.

I asked her if she had gone to the police with this information and she said, "Yes, but there was no evidence and the authorities would not probe any deeper." She was extremely agitated, as one would expect any mother to be who believed her son was murdered. She made the threat that if justice weren't served, she would take things into her own hands.

And she had the hands to do it.

If this was a suicide, there was an ethical question about whether I should be involved in providing a Christian burial service. At the time it was a theological consideration that if someone took their own life, it was a sign of lack of faith and trust in God and therefore a Christian funeral was not appropriate. So I called a neighboring pastor whose council I trusted. As the Lord directs things, he was acquainted with the couple and had provided marriage counseling for them on several occasions. He filled me in about their marriage relationship. He told me that it was entirely possible for the husband in his simple but strong faith, realizing that his wife loved another man, to have committed suicide in order to do the "gentlemanly thing."

Could it be that this man was thinking that his wife and children would be better off in the care of someone who could provide a better life style? Had he thought through the situation and come to the conclusion that with the addition of his insurance money, his wife and children would be better off? Had he truly committed suicide?

Or was he murdered?

It was hard for me to identify with such thinking. If the man didn't commit suicide because of lack of faith or if he was murdered, either way, it gave me the rationale to provide a Christian funeral.

As I conducted the funeral there was an uneasy feeling in the pit of my stomach that things could get out of hand. I wasn't sure how the dead man's mother might react in her grief and anger. The dead man's wife sat on one side of the church with her friend comforting her and his parents on the other. There were a lot of daggery stares being aimed at each other, but things remained calm through the funeral service.

A week following the funeral, I decided to drive over to the widow's home and see how she and her young children were coping. It was coincidental that an agent for the husband's life insurance company had arrived before I did and they were going over the payment of the insurance. I sat in the living room and entertained the widow's two daughters who were four and six. I overheard the agent say that there was no exclusion in case of suicide and that the full benefit would be paid. The widow was to receive the check in a week to ten days.

But what really set me on edge was what the older girl told me. She asked me, "Do you know why my Daddy died?" I really didn't want to answer that question, so I said, "No, I don't. Do you?" Then she dropped the bombshell on me, "Mommy and Bill got rid of Daddy so they could get married."

Now what does one do with such inside information?

I surely did not want to tell the dead man's mother and have another murder on my hands. The best action I could take was to report to the authorities what the little girl told me.

I heard no more about this situation for several weeks. Still curious, I called the county attorney's office and was told that they wouldn't reopen the case on the testimony of a six-year old girl because she was too young to make a credible witness.

Case closed!

Later that summer a pastor assumed the ministry of that congregation and in the business of my own ministry, I lost track of what was happening there. My thoughts occasionally return to that situation and I wonder just what did happen. I often think that with the modern science of crime scene investigation and DNA testing of today authorities could piece together exactly what happened in the barn that night.

For now only the Lord, the wife, and Bill know for sure.

Chapter 7 – A Community Deals with Vietnam

"He (Jesus) will judge between the nations and settle disputes for many peoples. They will beat their swords into plowshares and their spears into pruning hooks. Nation will not take up sword against nation, nor will they train for war anymore." Isaiah 2:4

Our Lord guides the direction of our lives in ways that we never anticipate. He is a great God whose wisdom far exceeds our own. And because He is so wise, we must trust in His direction even though it goes beyond our comprehension. For, if we could understand the reasoning of God, He would be like us and that would be scary. But because He is God and all wise, we must trust in Him in all things and suppress our need to ask the question, "Why Lord?"

Our nation was in the midst of the war in Vietnam and two marines from Columbia were serving in that war-torn country. One marine was a strapping young man of athletic build. He stood an imposing 6 foot 5 inches tall with broad shoulders and was in excellent physical shape. One would think that if anyone could take care of himself and return home it would be Lance Corporal Lenny Craig. The other marine was more slightly built and was about 5 foot 10 inches tall. Captain Robert Moony was more of a student than an athlete. If one had to choose, he was a less likely candidate to return home a decorated war hero.

I was just pulling into the driveway after returning home from a meeting at Peace Church in Hecla. The headlights of my car flashed on a vehicle parked next to the parsonage and, as they illuminated the car, it started up and sped away. I recognized the car as belonging to Elnora, Robert's mother. I knew she must be troubled about something and that I must have startled her. I followed her to her home a few blocks away, coaxed her into my warmer car and asked her what was bothering her. Obviously filled with a mother's worry, she answered, "I haven't heard from Robert! It is not like him not to write. Usually I get a letter each week and it's been over a month. I have a premonition that something terrible has happened to him. I'm just so afraid!"

"Why did you drive off when I pulled in the yard?" I asked.

"I needed to talk to someone and I thought of you, Pastor. But, when I saw you weren't home, I just sat there in my car for a while. When you came home so late, I was startled and I didn't want to bother you, so I drove off."

I visited with her for a while trying to calm her shattered nerves by reassuring her with positive comments. "Maybe Robert's letters have been held up in the mail. In the next few days you will probably receive several."

She was not easy to comfort because her motherly intuition was telling her something terrible had happened.

We prayed for Robert, that the Lord was watching over him to keep him safe and that she would soon receive a letter saying that he was all right.

Elnora's hopes were not encouraged when the days passed and she still didn't hear from her son.

Able and Iris Craig, however, had to face the scene of two marines in full dress uniform approaching their front door. They were notified that Lenny had been killed in action and his body was being shipped back to Columbia for burial

The report given by the marines was not very comforting. They reviewed the battle in which Lenny died. Lenny and his platoon had bravely taken a hill near Da Nang in the midst of fierce fighting. But it wasn't long before they discovered that they had been suckered in. They were surrounded by Vietcong and were receiving heavy fire and taking many casualties. They radioed frantically for air support but it didn't get there in time. The Vietcong battered the hill with mortar shells until not one marine was left alive.

Able and Iris were devastated.

I was with them at the time of their first viewing of Lenny's body in the coffin. He was such a big man that his shoulders touched each side of the casket. Also, he was so tall that his head was bent in an uncomfortable looking position at the head of the open coffin. It was a heart-wrenching scene as mother and father gazed at their son, remembering him so full of life. In her grief, Iris wanted to reach into the coffin and touch her son but a sheet of clear Plexiglas sealed the casket and prevented any human contact. Iris asked the funeral director if the barrier might be removed, even for a few minutes, so she could hold him in her arms and readjust his position. The funeral director advised against it because her son's body had been lying in the casket a long time and would be too fragile.

A handsome young marine with a boyish face, who was about Lenny's age, was assigned to accompany the body to Columbia and remain with it through burial. He was very compassionate and connected so completely with the grieving parents that they were ready to adopt him as their own. They wished he could be a replacement for Lenny, but, of course, no one could. He stayed in contact with Able and Iris for some time following the funeral.

Lenny and his mother were members of the Congregational Church in Columbia. His father was a member of our Lutheran church. The funeral was expected to be a wonderful outpouring of community support with a large attendance, so the family requested the use of our church, which was the larger of the two. Of course, permission was given. Lenny's pastor conducted the service.

On the day of the funeral, our church was filled to overflowing. Mourners and supporters from the surrounding community filled the church and basement, where we had set up a speaker system so everyone could hear the service. The church was so packed that people had to stand outside to demonstrate their care and support for the family.

Elnora joined the mourners carrying her own fear and grief inside her aching heart. Her face was drawn and pale as she moved through the line of people offering condolences to the family. All the while, she prayed that she would not have to endure a similar ordeal in the near future. She kept her grief private, carrying her burden deep inside her heart. She put on a cheerful front, not wanting her fear to cast a shadow over the observance for Lenny nor detract from comfort for his family.

The day following the funeral the mail brought her the good news she had been awaiting. Three letters from Robert arrived dated several days apart.

Elnora couldn't wait to share them with me.

The first letter contained the usual information of his daily activities. The last two revealed a very different account of his day. He wrote about a marine unit that suffered heavy casualties and how he and his men flew in on helicopters to evacuate the wounded. When the choppers landed in the clearing the Vietcong had them surrounded. In the midst of heavy fire, Robert and his men continued the evacuation. Some of his men were wounded in the onslaught, but they continued the mission until everyone was removed.

By the grace of God Robert was not injured.

Elnora could not contain her joy. Half laughing and half crying, she thanked me for talking to her that night and for offering a prayer that helped her hold on in faith until she heard from her son.

For his bravery in rescuing his comrades in the face of fierce enemy fire, Robert received the bronze star. As so many men returning from Vietnam never spoke about their heroism, Robert didn't speak about his experiences there or his heroism either. So his bravery went unsung in the community.

Here were two families and two outcomes. Lenny's mother and father mourned the loss of a wonderful son, but they also gave thanks to God for the years that they had with him. They were cheered by the powerful outpouring of support shown by the care of the Columbia community. That comforted them for a long time.

Elnora rejoiced that Robert returned home safely. It was obvious to me that God knew she needed someone to care for her in her later years. Robert was glad to be home too, surrounded by a close-knit community that cared about its own and received him without the stigma attached to so many troops returning from Vietnam.

What was the difference between these two young marines that the outcome was so different? Christians don't believe in fate. Obviously God allowed Lenny to be taken to heaven while he allowed Robert to come home. But why was there this difference?

Did God know more than we did?

Obviously!

But what did He know?

We'll never know.

But that's all right. We just need to trust and believe that He knows what's best for those who believe in Him. We must keep holding on to our Lord's promise in Holy Scripture that, "All things work together for good to those who love God and who are called by his purpose."

Chapter 8 – Unforgettable Otto

"'For this son of mine was dead and is alive again: he was lost and is found.' So they began to celebrate." St. Luke 15:24

When a pastor plays an instrumental role in bringing a person back into the fold of the Lord and the church it's very rewarding.

There are certain colorful people that you never forget.

His name was Otto.

He was the town drunk.

The only time anyone saw him was when he was on his way to or from the tavern with a brown paper bag containing his favorite brew.

If you ever wanted to use someone's face to depict that of a captain of the sea, you would pick Otto's. He had a weathered, round face with rosy cheeks and a button nose that would look convincing peaking through a Santa Clause beard. His dark curly hair was matted and dirty but the corners of his mouth were drawn up in an impish smile and his eyes twinkled all the way to his little crows feet wrinkles,

He was somewhat shy and avoided people. As I came to discover, this was due more to a feeling of guilt for his drinking habit than from a dislike of them. He wore dark clothing that hung on him and during the cold weather covered everything with a black cloth dress coat. He gave off an aroma -- a not totally offensive mixture of booze and sweet smelling pipe tobacco. And he walked with a determined walk, leaning forward as if into the wind.

Otto lived across the street from the church in a small home owned by his cousin and his wife. One day as the cousin and I were walking back from the post office, he just happened to mention that at one time Otto attended the Lutheran Church. I caught the unspoken suggestion to get him back into the faith and away from his sinful drinking habit. So, when I saw Otto returning from his favorite shopping spree with his bag under his arm, it was time to strike.

As I approached him he seemed nervous and protective about the contents of his package and he shifted it to the arm that was away from me.

"Hi Otto! How are you today?"

Otto shifted on his feet nervously and looked at the sky. "Oh I guess I'm all right. We could use some rain though."

He tried to direct the conversation to something non-threatening. But I was not about to be sidetracked from my appointed duty.

"Hey Otto! I understand that you used to go to the Lutheran Church. Is that right?"

"Oh, that was a long time ago."

"Well why don't you come back? Church is at 9 A.M. on Sunday," I shot back at him.

"Well, I'll tell you Pastor," and I knew the excuse was coming. "I don't think the folks at your church would appreciate my showing up there."

"Why not?'

"Well because of my reputation in town and I don't have any nice clothes either."

I formed my reply quickly. "Otto you might be surprised. I'm sure most of them would be very happy if you came to church. I know that they would receive you with great joy and would welcome you with open arms. Just come Sunday and you can see for yourself."

"Pastor, I know these people. They don't accept me and they don't approve of how I live my life!"

Now I was getting impatient with him and his excuses and, as I turned to walk away, I gave him my parting shot.

"Otto, you can make all of the excuses you like, but some day you will enter the church and I just hope it isn't going to be feet first." And I walked away.

I guess that Otto got my gist because the following Sunday morning, I couldn't believe my eyes. Sitting all alone in the balcony in the back of the church was Otto. He had spirited in after church had started and left before anyone saw him, but I knew he was there. I was so excited and wanted to let him know that I saw him that I stared right at him at the same time I was trying to read from the Bible.

I smiled at him.

He smiled back and I completely lost my place in the Bible reading.

Monday morning I went to see Otto to tell him how thankful I was that he had attended church. When I knocked on the door his cousin answered and told me that he had kicked him out of the house a week before because he was drunk and belligerent and he was getting to be a problem. His wife had given him an ultimatum.

"Either Otto goes or I do. Now which is it?"

Now I understood why he wanted me to get Otto back into church.

Later I found out that Otto was sleeping in an empty chicken coup behind Marta Crane's house about a block away. It was late in October and the nights were getting very chilly and the temperature was closing in on freezing.

During my investigation to locate Otto, by chance, I ran into "Speed" and Hanna Crane who were his distant relatives and good members of the church. They wanted to tell me that they felt guilty as a result of the sermon I preached that previous Sunday on the Parable of the Good Samaritan from Luke 10:25-37. They knew about Otto's plight and had compassion on him. They cleaned up a little three-room cottage that they used to store stuff in and set him up in it complete with furniture. It was wonderful to discover that a sermon had such an immediate positive impact.

I had to go see how Otto was doing in his new surroundings. I found him in a cozy little cabin that just fit his needs. It had cleaned up very well and had a rustic hominess about it. There were three rooms made up of a cozy living room, an efficiency kitchen and an indoor "biffy," as Otto called it. He was so proud of his little place and exceedingly grateful to Speed and Anna for letting him live there. I think part of the reason was that it was even closer to the tavern where he bought his booze.

Otto became regular in his church attendance still taking his perch in the balcony on Sundays. Gradually more of the members of the church spotted him in the balcony as they were returning to their seats after receiving communion at the altar. They mad a big fuss over him when he came down and he was grateful for the way in which the church members received him.

But I noticed that he never attended Holy Communion.

I asked him, "Why?"

"I'm too embarrassed to come down from the balcony and walk down the center aisle. I have a little trouble walking in a straight line sometimes. And I don't feel comfortable rubbing shoulders with the upstanding members."

"I understand. Otto. I'll bring you communion at your place".

A few days later I showed up at his doorstep with my communion case. Otto welcomed me and we visited for a while and then I set up for Holy Communion. As we went through the communion service I came to the place where it was time to give him the bread and wine. Otto stood up, which surprised me, and with tears streaming down his ruddy cheeks he received Christ's forgiveness in the sacrament for the first time in years.

It was a touching experience for me, as I had never seen anyone cry as they received the sacrament. Even before I had completed the closing prayer and the benediction, Otto wiped the tears of joy from his eyes and reached out to shake my hand in appreciation.

"It has been so long ago that I have received the Lord's Supper that I can't even remember when. But it felt so good. It was just like old times. I really needed it. Thank you Pastor for bringing it to me."

And it was my joy to bring him the Lord's forgiveness on a regular basis after that.

About a year later, when the air was getting chilly again and it was time for me to bottle my annual batch of choke cherry wine, it was Otto's birthday. Mary and Deloris, a friend and member of the church came up with the idea of making a birthday lunch for Otto complete with a birthday cake.

I wondered what I could give him that would be something special. It was early in my ministry and I was still wet behind the ears as far as understanding alcoholism and how to deal with it. But I was bottling my wine and it seemed like a great idea to give him a bottle with the stern warning to drink it judiciously. I believed that because of his respect for me it might help him with his drinking problem.

I took the bottle of wine over to him at about 10 A.M. and left it with the strict encouragement to enjoy it a little at a time.

I was not too sure about how Otto would handle the wine and my direction. So, when the ladies took the birthday lunch over to him, I asked Mary to look for the bottle of wine and see how much he drank.

She returned with the report that it was almost half gone by noon.

My heart sank and I felt I had not helped Otto at all but had contributed to his problem.

But Mary said that he had given them an excuse that when he opened the bottle the wine fizzed all over the floor and he had spent the morning on his hands and knees scrubbing it up.

I believed that had to be a cover up, but Mary said that the floor did look freshly scrubbed and in places was still drying.

That night as Mary and I were getting ready for bed, suddenly there was what sounded like a gunshot.

It was close.

"Mary get down on the floor!" I ordered. "Someone's shooting at us!"

As we lay on the floor, I heard a similar, cracking sound, but this time I could tell that it was coming from our basement. Dressed in my pajamas, I went down to investigate and followed the sound to the fruit cellar where I had just stashed my supply of freshly bottled wine.

As soon as I opened the door things became clear. The bottles of wine were exploding. I had used the empty wine bottles from the communion wine at the church and they were not strong enough for the pressure that was building up inside.

A light went on in my head and I realized that the vent on the barrel in which I was brewing my wine must have been plugged and the bubbles from the fermenting wine were forced back into the brew.

I had, unwittingly, made champagne!

I released the pressure on all of the remaining bottles and as I did so about half of the liquid sprayed out all over me. I was a pretty sticky mess by the time I was all done, but I had a sense of relief as I came upstairs.

"Mary, Otto didn't drink all that wine! When he opened the bottle it did fizz all over! It's champagne and I am glad!"

As the years passed, Otto's health failed to the point that he could not tolerate alcohol anymore. The Lord took care of his drinking problem for him. But Otto still came to church. One day he fell gravely ill with a stroke and was taken to the hospital. He slipped into a coma from which he never regained consciousness.

The Lord took him to heaven and I had his funeral at church. I left specific instructions with the funeral director, that when Otto's casket was brought into the church, he was to make sure that they brought his body in "head" first.

It is a rare success when a pastor can reach a person who is enjoying their sinful ways and heading away from the Lord. But with God's help leading my fumbling attempts, Otto returned to a strong faith in Jesus as his Savior who loved him just as he was.

I have no doubt that Otto is now rejoicing with his Lord in the glory of heaven drinking the nectar of eternal life.

Chapter 9 - Communion in Technicolor and other Strange Things.

"Ascribe to the Lord the glory due his name; worship the Lord in the splendor of his holiness." Psalm 29:2

Two very important rules in the ministry are never loose your cool and never ever lose your sense of humor. You may wonder how that applies to the perfunctory distribution of Holy Communion, but it does.

Writing about giving Holy Communion to Otto in the last chapter reminded me of my student ministry days in St. Louis. People there were super concerned about offensive breath odor. Almost everyone sucked on a breath mint or some mouth freshener.

That reality struck home my first time distributing the bread at communion. As I went down the line people would stick out their tongue for me to place the communion wafer on it

I was surprised that the first tongue was bright green.

The second tongue was red.

After that the colors came one after the other in a myriad of

black,
blue,
red,
green

in a random rotation. I fully expected someone to stick out his or her tongue with the color culprit still glued to it.

I had to suppress my laughter as I realized that we were having Holy Communion in Technicolor.

The church in Columbia had its own particular process of distributing communion. In the winter with the forced air furnace blasting, the air would dry out and static electric shock was a common experience. The church had a maroon wool carpet that ran down the center aisle. This did nothing to improve the static problem as people shuffled forward for communion.

Before I began to distribute communion, I would touch my ankle to a strategically placed heat register so that I wouldn't give some unexpected member a jolt of static electricity. The contact with the register gave me a slight shock, but it usually spared the communicant.

But sometimes even the best of plans fail and it was a "shock" to say the least.

A gentleman got up from the very last row in the church and shuffled down the full length of that wool carpet and he ended up being the person farthest away from the heat register. By the time I got to him with the bread, I was charged and he was almost glowing. As I reached out to place the communion wafer on his tongue, a static-electric charge arced a full three inches from my finger to his out-stretched tongue. The man's head recoiled, his eyes rolled around and he began to tear up.

He looked at me with eyes that questioned, *why me?* In a stroke of what I considered genius I laid my hand on his head in blessing and said, "Receive the Holy Spirit!"

After that, the man never shuffled his feet and he moved up to the front row.

There was another challenge of administering communion at St. John's. It had to do with a short and very rotund lady in the congregation. She introduced herself to me as the fattest lady in the congregation. I had to agree, but not openly.

To make matters worse, it appeared like her head was connected to her body without a neck. She was quite buxom and, on top of everything, she wore dresses that revealed her cavernous cleavage.

This made it difficult to get the communion cup to her lips without either pushing on her bosom or spilling the wine down her front. So, before beginning the distribution, I looked over the congregation in order to locate her and planned how I might have the cup almost empty by the time she came to the communion rail. I timed it right <u>most</u> of the time.

It may look like a cinch to distribute communion, but it takes an eight-year degree and lots of experience to do it right. One learns to tailor the distribution to each person.

The congregation where I retired had each communicant take their own elements from trays put in front of them.

That took all the fun and challenge out of communion distribution.

Chapter 10 – The Blizzard of 1966

"The wind blows wherever it pleases. You hear its sound, but you cannot tell where it comes from or where it is going. So it is with everyone born of the Spirit." St. John 3:8

Many situations can upset plans for ministry on any given day but one that is not often considered is the weather. On days during which a blizzard was raging outdoors, I gladly used the time to catch up on comfy indoor tasks such as, studying, writing sermons or working on the church annual report.

In Columbia, South Dakota, those days came often.

The first winter we lived in Columbia we received our initiation. It was March of 1966. The forecast was for a fierce three-day blizzard starting on Friday, the day I usually write my sermon.

Friday dawned and the weather was partly cloudy and didn't appear to hold in store what the weatherman was forecasting. But I just could not sit down and concentrate on writing my sermon. I sat at my desk for a few minutes and would study the text and then jump to my feet and look out the window checking the weather for just one furtive little snowflake that would confirm the prediction. I felt like a nervous, caged lion expecting something sinister to happen. After all, if the storm were to hit as fiercely as predicted, there certainly would be no church on Sunday, so why exercise the futility of writing a sermon?

On the other hand if no storm developed, or it was not as bad as predicted, I would be in a pickle on Sunday if I hadn't prepared a sermon. Being fresh out of the seminary, I didn't have a "barrel" of sermons that I could draw from in case of emergency.

I waited. I sat at my desk and gazed out the window. I paced. I sat down again to work on my sermon but no inspiration came. I wasted the whole day without accomplishing a thing.

Not one snowflake appeared.

That night while I got ready for bed I was still looking out the window for the first sign of a change in the weather. The wind had picked up and was howling and rattling the windows. The electric wires that were attached to the parsonage would hum when the wind was at least 30 miles per hour. They were giving a sustained humming that sounded like an eighteen-wheel truck traveling 70 miles an hour past our parsonage.

Still there was no snow.

Mary and I cuddled in bed as best we could against the sound of the rattling windows and the moaning sounds of the old two-story house that was built in 1907. Cuddling was not as easy as normal in those days because Mary was in her 8th month of pregnancy with our first child.

During the night while we slept the storm hit with a vengeance. There would be no church services on Sunday!

Daylight revealed that the howling winds had carried not only one snowflake, but also a nation of them all congregating in piles, called drifts. Our electric power had gone out and therefore our furnace was rendered useless and we were without heat. I wondered how long we could stay in our cozy bed before we had to take action for self-preservation.

The ring of the telephone shocked me into the realization that the time had come. I grabbed for a robe and slippers and dashed down the steep flight of stairs to answer the complaining sound. It was Darlene, she and her husband, Will, and three children lived just two houses away from us on other side of our church. She said they had heat because they used an oil heater in their home and that we should bundle up and come over.

That was no easy task. The easy part was bundling up. But getting there was a different story. The drifts had gathered into 4 and 5 feet piles making the trek from our back door to theirs somewhat of a challenge. What made things worse was Mary's center of gravity was shifted, making her balance far from that of a tightrope walker. It was hard enough for me to get through the big drifts, but it was a major accomplishment to help her plow thought as well. But leaning into the force of the snow-filled wind and checking our bearings occasionally to make sure that we were headed in the right direction, we finally made it cold and wet and looking like tiny abominable snowmen.

Their cozy home was warm and inviting. The smell of coffee and hot food filled our senses as soon as we opened the door. We stripped off our wet clothes and joined the family for breakfast. It was then that we realized the wonderful generosity of this family. They had also taken in Millie, the 85 year-old lady who lived between their house and the church.

Millie was not artificial in any sense of the word. She was forthright in sharing what was on her mind, and no one ever had doubts as to what was on it. She loved her Lord and her church dearly and worked hard to make sure that it succeeded in every way.

Millie was the first person Mary and I met when we came to visit the church in Columbia before assuming our ministry duties.

While we were touring the parsonage, she asked me, "Can you preach in German?" "Not very well," was my response. "If I tried, you wouldn't want to hear another sermon like it."

"Can you play the organ, then?"

"No."

"Then what can you do?"

Our host, Will, had just appeared on the scene to meet the new pastoral couple and he hung his head in embarrassed unbelief at Tillie's brazen-ness.

Another impromptu guest on that snowy morning was Will's brother, Harry, who had been bowling in nearby Aberdeen. He had just barely made it through the storm to Will's house. He lived out in the country with his mother another 5 miles away.

We stayed with Will and Marlys and their extended family for two nights sharing food, fun and laughter. The howling wind and circling snow outside was a distant consideration compared to the warm hospitality we received and the friendship we developed in the confines of their home.

Millie wouldn't stay overnight. We could have made room for her to sleep somewhere. Will and Marlys had given up their bed for Mary and me. The children already had given up their beds and were sleeping on the floor. But Millie felt compelled to go home at night. She needed the security of her own bed and wanted to keep guard on her home. She said convincingly, "I'll be just fine because I have lots of blankets and I will hold up in my bedroom with some burning candles to keep me from freezing."

It was the thought of those candles burning with her sleeping near by that bothered me. I offered to walk with her next door to make sure that she got home all right. Millie showed me how she would take care of herself. The double bed she slept in practically filled her little bedroom. There was barely enough room to walk around it to put the sheets on. It was piled a foot high with a myriad of covers consisting of blankets, quilts, afghans and a feather comforter.

I thought that if she survived the cold of the night she might die of suffocation.

What worried me the most was the 57 varieties of candles she had strewn on every square inch of remaining space in that bedroom. It looked like a shrine to the god of fire. If Millie didn't freeze to death, or smother under the weight of the covers, surely she would be a victim of fire. But she showed up each morning looking rested from her night's ordeal. I believe my prayers had something to do with her getting safely through the night.

It was, however, Will's brother that my heart went out too the most. He had to be in a most embarrassing situation. He was a member of our church but never attended. Now he was cooped up in the little house, held captive by a raging blizzard with the "pastor" having no way of escape. To pass the time we played cards for hours on end, but never once did I mention to Harry his truancy from worship at church. I let his conscience do the dirty work. At least I hoped his feeling of guilt was working overtime on him. If he was feeling a bit sheepish, his Whist game didn't show any preoccupation.

Harry did show up at church on sparse occasions after that, but I felt that it was due more to the fact that food was being served and his mother refused to fix him anything to eat at home that he came. Perhaps he also felt more comfortable after establishing a relationship with this new pastor that he could easily beat at cards.

But where my evangelism technique failed, his marriage two years later succeeded in getting Harry to church more regularly. Never underestimate the encouragement of a faithful Christian spouse, whether it is in the form of Law or Gospel.

It works. So, don't knock it!

The blizzard ended in the wee hours of Monday morning. The sun came up and Millie arose from her flaming inferno to enjoy another day. It was also time to let Harry quit squirming and go check on how his and Will's mother was doing out in the country.

The three of us piled into Will's pickup truck and headed for her farmhouse. We took a circuitous route, which Will knew we would encounter the least snowdrifts. As we bounced along over the snow covered roads, there were numerous exclamations and fingers pointing out how the force of the storm had blown the snow past the tree lined shelter belts and piled it up on the leeward side. Drifts were often 10 to 12 feet high.

After what seemed like a short trip because of all the amazing snowy sights we saw, but in reality took longer than normal, we arrived at where we knew the farmhouse stood. We knew it had to be there from the other landmarks.

But it was nowhere to be seen. All that was there was a gigantic snowdrift.

We got out of the truck and with great wonder headed in the direction that the house should be. The drifts were hard packed enough to walk on and as I made my way over a large one, I tripped on something sticking out of the snow. Looking back with puzzled eyes, I focused on two inches of radio antenna sticking out of the snow. I had just walked over a pickup truck that was completely buried except for that little section of antenna.

Once on the other side of that snowdrift, we could see the roof of the house. The snow had blown so hard threw the shelterbelt that it had swirled around the house and buried the front and back doors and every window was covered.

We walked from the snowdrift to the roof of the house and began to dig with our hands to get to the front door. Will went back to the truck to get a shovel to make the job go quicker. All the time we dug, we yelled to their mother inside believing that she must be in a panic thinking that the whole area was buried in 15 feet of snow.

By the time we got the door open and scrambled into the house, we found Will and Harry's mother sitting in her rocking chair in her heavy blue sweater with the potbellied stove almost red hot. She was not anxious at all. She said, " I just figured that everybody's house was covered like this and, it being March, that I would have to wait for spring to see the neighbors. I had enough firewood and food around here to get me to the middle of April if I conserved a little. I had my Bible and some other things to read to keep me occupied until then. I wasn't worried at all. I knew someone would come get me out sooner or later."

She was right.

By the middle of April, most of the snow had melted. The little town of Columbia was almost an island as a result of the snowmelt flowing into the normally sanguine James River, which cupped the town in its caressing hand.

While we were in the midst of the raging storm, I considered our options if Mary went into early labor. Now there was a new concern, if the bridge leading out of Columbia over the river were to become submerged, how would I get Mary to the hospital in Aberdeen?

The situation must have come up before, because Will had a ready answer to that question. He said, "A car will drive her to the edge of the floodwater then a boat would take her across the swollen river and another car would be waiting on the other side to transport her to the hospital."

It seemed simple enough. The only problem with that solution was that Mary didn't like deep, rushing water very much.

We trusted in the Lord! He takes care of all things. The floodwater never covered the bridge, so in the early morning darkness of April 15th, when Mary woke me and said it was time to go to the hospital, we made the 20-mile trip without incident.

It was a good thing my taxes were prepared because that was the last thing on my mind.

Mary was taken into the delivery room at around 11:00 A.M. and I occupied the fathers' waiting room doing the usual expectant father thing, pacing. Realizing that my pacing was not helping anyone, I plunked down on the couch and promptly fell asleep. I awoke with a start 75 minutes later wondering if I missed anything. All was quiet and I was becoming concerned, so I went to the delivery room door. There was half-an-inch gap between the double doors through which I could see movement and hear sounds. To protect my nose from being broken if someone opened the door, I wedged my shoe against the bottom. From what I could hear there was no birth yet. But the curious sound of women's voices reached my ear. They were chanting, "Come baby, come! Come baby, come!" It was the student nurses who were observing the birth and were concerned that they might miss their lunch.

Lisa came into the world at 12:29 high and dry.

Well mostly dry.

Daughters Lisa and Lori with Skippy after a snowstorm.

Chapter 11 – Dreaming of a White Christmas

"You say...in the morning, 'Today it will be stormy, for the sky is red and overcast. You know how to interpret the appearance of the sky, but you cannot interpret the sign of the times." St. Matthew 16:3

It snowed a lot in Columbia. But I was quite confident of my winter weather driving skills gained from Minnesota where I grew up. That sometimes got me into trouble when, even armed with a heavy car and snow tires with studs, I would plunge into a snowdrift and get stuck. Often I would get high centered and with my wheels spinning off the ground there was nothing I could do. So I would trudge through the snow to the nearest farmhouse and someone would get a tractor and pull me out.

It was our first Christmas in Columbia but instead of singing, "I'm Dreaming of a White Christmas," the weather decided to play a little trick on us so that we changed our song to "The Skater's Waltz." Instead of snowing it rained and froze. Everything was a skating rink for two weeks, especially the roads that were crowned for water drainage. That made things worse because if one tried to stop they would slowly slide off into the ditch anyway.

Where ever people gathered the conversation would turn to how many times they slid into the ditch and what harrowing experience got them there. It was good that no one ever got hurt that we knew of.

I was proud that, with all the driving I did, I had not gone into the ditch once.

But pride goes before the fall.

It was early on Sunday morning and the first time we had seen the sun for a week. Mary and I were driving to Peace Lutheran Church 20 miles north of Columbia. It was slippery and the sun was just beginning to melt the ice on the roads, which made everything even more dangerous. I was driving very cautiously trying to preserve my perfect record of ditchless-ness. As I navigated the turn just before coming to the church, looming ominously ahead of me was the car of some older members who were creeping along very slowly.

Before I knew it, we were right on their tail. As we came up on their car, I realized that hitting my brakes would send us into a skid that would certainly throw us into the ditch. The thought of ruining my spotless driving record flashed before my eyes. That, however, wasn't as important as not plowing into the back of a member's car and pushing them into the ditch, perhaps causing injury to them or us or both.

My plan was to ease past them on the left and gradually cut back onto the right side of the road then gradually slow down for the turn into the church parking lot.

It was a great plan, but poorly executed.

Just as we pulled even with the car, the driver realized that we were right next to him. He looked at us in shock as we passed on his left, and he involuntarily turned his steering wheel in the direction he was looking. Our cars were neck and neck and Mary and he were looking at each other with only about two feet separating their noses.

I was keeping my eyes on the road as the other driver gradually brought his vehicle back into the right lane.

I heaved a sigh of relief too soon.

We had passed, but up ahead was a patch of road that was melting. I knew that it was going to be a problem. As I inched the car back into the right lane we hit that patch of melted ice and lost control of the car.

Our car fishtailed to the right and I cranked the wheel to the right and straightened her out. But now we were beginning to fishtail to the left.

I turned the wheel to the left and brought the car around again. Only it didn't straighten out. Instead, we made a complete 360-degree counter clockwise circle and backed into the ditch directly in front of the church. The car behind us navigated the patch of ice without incident and passed our car as it plunged into the ditch with snow flying.

Since the sun was out, there were half-a-dozen men of the church standing outside taking the last drags of their cigarettes before church.

Everything seemed to move in slow motion as we hit the ditch. Once we came to a stop in the bottom I could see the men's faces, which were clearly etched into my mind. They were devoid of any concern, but registered an amusement and satisfaction that finally the pastor had succumbed the to icy roads and made his dramatic entry into the ditch. If they had signs with them they would have rated our dive into the ditch with 5.7, 5.8, 5.7, 5.9, 5.8 and 5.9 throwing out the highest and lowest scores.

Fortunately, there was not a lot snow in the ditch, which allowed us to drive 50 yards to the next approach and climb back on the highway. This time we were able to maneuver around the melting spot to turn off of the skating rink road into the church parking lot.

As we climbed out of the car, I was a little shaky and Mary was relieved that we made it. The men, who had extinguished their smokes, did not say a word as we entered the church, but their grins said everything.

The next Christmas we got the snow we sing about—"I'm Dreaming of a White Christmas."

As our family - which now included our daughter, Lisa and my mother, who was visiting us from St. Paul - was getting dressed for the Christmas Eve service, it began to snow in the most beautiful way. Big fluffy flakes that looked more like feathers floated down with absolutely no wind. It seemed like it took the snowflakes an eternity to drift from the sky above. They landed on everything and stuck there so that fence posts and anything that could hold snow quickly had a stack of it.

By the time I walked the 60 yards to the church, everything had been transformed into a winter wonderland. The snow had piled up on the fence posts to a depth of six inches. Still no wind blew and, in the fading light of dusk, the snow sparkled like diamonds.

I thought it was the most beautiful Christmas Eve I had ever seen.

I was to start the Christmas worship service at St. John's, which was always packed, and then turn it over to the Sunday school children for their pageant. Then I would slip out, meet Lisa and my mother at the car, and drive north to Peace Church for their service. The school principal was to conclude the service at St. John's with the benediction.

Things didn't go quite according to the plan.

By the time the service was in progress, darkness had fallen and a steady wind was blowing that beautiful snow into fluffy drifts.

Lisa, my mother and I drove north and it wasn't too difficult to maneuver in the snow because it was so fluffy. But when we got to the edge of town and left behind the protection of the trees, the wind picked up and was piling up great drifts.

It took me only a half-mile of driving before I came to two realizations. One, it was too treacherous to go farther, and two, at the rate I was traveling, I would never get to the service at Peace in time. So I looked for a place to turn around.

We came to a farmyard and could see some lights through the blowing snow. I hoped that I could use their phone to call someone at Peace to let them know that we couldn't make it. The family was in the midst of opening their Christmas presents, but they were kind enough to take a hiatus and let me make a phone call. The members I called had already left for church and the church had no phone, but I figured they would get the "drift" of why we didn't make it.

We headed back to Columbia, pulled the car into the garage and I made sure that Lisa and my mother got safely into the house. Then I headed to the church to warn the members about the raging storm outside.

The Sunday school pageant was coming to an end, so I quickly donned my gown and took my seat in the chancel, just like I never left. Only the principal seemed surprised that I had returned.

I stood up to pronounce the benediction and then gave the warning that there was a strong snowstorm blowing outside even though it wasn't evident inside. Then I told the people, "The weather report that I heard on the car radio said that the storm would blow over in another hour." "Please," I said, "stay at the church or in town with relatives until the storm lets up."

I could hear a few scattered scoffs that communicated, "Chicken Pastor! He doesn't know what a "real" snowstorm is!"

It was when the first wave of people opened the back doors of the church and got their glimpse of the snow blowing horizontally that I heard the sounds of, "OOOOh!" And the full realization of what I was trying to tell them sunk in. Maybe this pastor did know what he was talking about.

Some people stayed in town and waited out the storm. Other used their ingenuity and formed car caravans of people heading in the same general direction. Some reported that when they got to the edge of town that the ditches were so filled with snow that the highway and ditch blended into one. A hardy volunteer walked in front of the cars feeling his way along on the road directing the cars that were inching along behind with their headlights getting lost in the blinding snow.

The snow stopped during the night and as the sun rose, its wondrous rays revealed a fresh white winter wonderland.

People began to arrive for the Christmas Day service and many comments expressed the beauty of God's creation that was covered with the purity of new fallen snow. The report given by members at the service was that the Lord had guided everyone home safely that night. No one was lost or even suffered frostbite.

I thanked God in prayer privately and in the worship service.

The consensus of all was that this young pastor knew what he was talking about and he should be listened to in the future.

Chapter 12 – The Humor of Hans and Isabel

"[There is] a time to weep and a time to laugh." Ecclesiastes 3:4

What makes the life of the minister so exciting is that no day is ever the same and the pastor never knows what he might run into. Hospital visitation can be one of the most versatile experiences a pastor can face. In one room you may be rejoicing with a couple on the birth of a healthy new baby and in the next room might be someone dying from cancer. The key to ministering to both situations appropriately is by making a quick shift in emotions rejoicing with the new parents and comforting the cancer patient.

I breathed in the fresh smells of autumn and reveled in the colors of that beautiful October day as I drove to St. Luke's Hospital in Aberdeen to visit a man in his sixties who had broken his leg. As I headed down the hall to his room I heard uproarious laughter from a man and woman echoing down the hall. As I appeared in the doorway the laughter stopped abruptly and was replaced with embarrassed looks on the faces of Hans and Isabel. In fact, the laughter stopped so quickly that it almost caught in their throats.

The snapshot that sticks in my mind was of Hans lying in the hospital bed with a cast from his toes to his hip, which was lifted about two feet off the bed by a system of traction pulleys. Isabel was sitting next to the bed on a straight back chair holding her husband's hand. The couple's mouths were still open from the laugh that died quickly when I came around the corner. It was obvious that I had startled them.

For the life of me, I couldn't figure out what could be so funny about a man with a broken leg that was suspended by traction. My puzzled expression must have been obvious because I didn't even have to ask what was so funny. Hans looked at Isabel and Isabel returned his look and she asked, "Should I tell him?" "Go ahead," he said with resignation.

Isabel began the story with Hans adding postscripts here and there. They related that they were reminiscing about a Halloween evening a year ago when Hans was engrossed in a Monday night football game on television while Isabel was handing out candy to the trick-or-treaters. Around 9 o'clock the regular ringing of the door bell with the shout of "Trick or treat! Money or eat!" had wound down. Isabel was looking for some attention from her husband, but he was engrossed in the game.

Everything became quiet in the house except for the sound of the game on TV, but Hans didn't notice because he was so engrossed in what he was watching. Suddenly his concentration was interrupted by the peal of the doorbell. "Isabel!" he shouted.

There was no answer.

"Isabel!" he shouted again. "There's some more trick-or-treaters at the door!"

No answer again.

Finally in disgust, Hans got up from his comfortable chair in front of the TV and backed toward the front door so he wouldn't miss a play. He blindly reached for the bowl of candy nearly knocking it over and opened the door ready to shove some of its contents into the awaiting sacks of the Trick-or-treaters. He took his eyes off the TV long enough to address the situation at hand.

But it wasn't Trick-or-treaters. It was Isabel at the front door in her fur coat. Just as Hans opened his mouth to ask how she got locked out, Isabel opened the front of her coat revealing her naked 65-year-old rotund body glistening in the light of the front porch.

"Trick or treat!" she said.

Hans grabbed her by the arm and said, "Get in here before some one sees you and calls the cops!"

Instantly Hans lost his interest in the football game and all the lights went out in the house. Isabel had succeeded in gaining her husband's undivided attention.

Now we all laughed together, but there was still an embarrassed glow on Isabel's cheeks and a satisfied twinkle in her eyes.

After our good laugh together, I asked how Hans wound up with the broken leg. That story was good for another belly laugh.

Hans related that he had been outside bringing in the apple harvest from the tree in the middle of the back yard. The ground was soft from an autumn rain and as Hans stretched beyond his limit to grab a beautiful red, ripe apple, one leg of the ladder began to sink into the ground. He knew better, but he was perched on the top step of the ladder holding onto the pail of apples with one hand and clutching a branch of the tree with the other. His center of gravity was going helter-skelter and he knew he was about to take a bad fall, so Hans called out to Isabel.

"Isabel! Help! Hurry!"

Isabel was washing dishes in the kitchen when she heard her husband shout. She looked out of her kitchen window and instantly grasped the severity of the situation. Isabel threw down her towel and moved as fast as her frame would allow. She tore down the steps to the back door and flung open the screen that separated her from her precariously perched husband. Then she barreled down the little hill in a race against time to save the portly figure whose ladder continued to sink in the soft ground

But she hadn't calculated very well.

Isabel arrived at the off kilter ladder before Hans fell, but as she grabbed on to steady it, she couldn't stop. Her momentum carried her on past her husband with the ladder still in her hands.

Hans said, in a mater-of-fact tone of voice, "She pulled it out from under me! I lost my grip on the tree limb and came crashing down on my leg and it broke."

Now we were all laughing again at the comical image, even though it wasn't funny at the time.

A nurse came in to see what all the laughing was about and I said to her, "You'd never believe it anyway." She checked the I.V. drip and left shrugging her shoulders while we laughed some more.

Altar at St. John's Lutheran Church

Chapter 13 – Tragedy on the Highway

"...a time to mourn." Ecclesiastes 3:4

A minister never knows when a tragedy might strike and it is hard to be prepared for one every minute. You hope and pray that one doesn't happen when you are involved somewhere else, but they do.

It was November, just six weeks before Christmas, and it was time for the annual over-night pastors' conference. This year it was in Gettysburg a little over 100 miles from home.

I made plans to carpool with a pastor friend, so I drove to Aberdeen to meet him and we rode together to Gettysburg in his car. The conference was rolling into the evening hours and was very interesting. I was so engrossed in the topic of "Ministry in the Rural World," that I didn't hear the telephone ring. It wasn't long before the host pastor tapped me on my shoulder and motioned me to come to the phone.

It was the anguished voice of Jill, a teenager from our church. "Pastor," she cried, "My mom was hit by a car. We're in the emergency room and I don't know what to do!"

I asked her, "What's your mother's condition?"

"I don't know! They won't let me see her."

"Is there a nurse there? Let me talk to her."

She put the nurse on the phone and I introduced myself as Jill's pastor. "Can you tell me how Helen is doing?" I asked. Helen was Hans and Isabel's daughter-in-law.

"Just a minute, I'll check."

The nurse returned to the phone in a few seconds and reported, "I'm sorry, but she has expired. She received extensive trauma internally, severe head lacerations and significant broken bones. We don't know how to tell her daughter."

"Please," I said, "Put her back on the phone. I'll tell her."

Jill came back on the phone. I could hear her voice quivering as she asked, "Is my mother going to be all right?"

"Jill, you have to be strong because the news isn't good. I'm sorry to have to tell you this, but the nurse told me that your mother has gone to heaven. She is in the arms of Jesus. The doctors did everything they could to save her, but she was too severely injured in the accident. Do you know where your father is? Can you reach him?"

"He's at a cattle sale. I think that my mother has the number of the sale barn in her purse."

"See if you can find the number and put in a call to him and have him come home right away. Tell him that your mother was severely injured in an accident and that you need him to come home immediately. I don't know how you located me in Gettysburg, but I'm glad you did. I'm here without my car, so I'm going to have to arrange a ride back home. Go home and I'll meet you and your family there as soon as I can get back."

"All right," and she hung up.

Now came the challenge of getting home. I announced the situation to the pastors and Pastor Gelling, a good friend, volunteered to take me back to Aberdeen where I had left my car.

I was so distressed about the accident and frustrated that I didn't have my own car so that I could leave right away and drive straight to the hospital, that every delay in making the trip back seemed to take forever. I blamed myself for riding with someone else. But I had no way of knowing that something like this would happen.

By the time I arrived at the house it was late and Terry, Helen's husband, had gotten home. Jill and her sister and brother sat together, huddled in embrace with their father. Their tear-filled faces wore expressions of gloom. Their mother was the type of person that kept the family running smoothly and now they were doomed to live without her. She reveled in doing little tasks for everyone in the family so that they could do the things they enjoyed.

Now she was gone.

My heart went out to this family that was suddenly adrift. I tried to comfort their loss with Scripture passages, relaying God's comfort and assurance that their mother was with Jesus in heaven. Somehow, with the coming of Christmas, it didn't seem like enough. I prayed with them and there was recognition of God's reassuring comfort on their faces, but their hurt ran deep.

Jill relayed what she knew of their mother's tragic accident. Helen and she decided to drive into town to do some Christmas shopping. Their car's engine had a history of quitting without warning. Terry had worked on it many times, but he couldn't find the problem. As fate would have it, the car stalled about a mile east of Aberdeen on Highway 12. Helen was able to pull off the road onto the shoulder. There was an implement dealership across the highway, so she left Jill in the car and went to call her husband. She hoped that he would leave the sale and pick them up on the way home. Terry added that she wasn't able to reach him.

Jill relayed how she watched her mother crossing the highway as she returned to the car. She crossed as far as the median and stopped, watching for traffic. Probably frustrated with their predicament and without thinking, she stepped into the westbound lane of the highway at the same time a car was approaching. The setting sun was shining in the driver's eyes blinding him and he didn't see her. Helen stepped right in front of him and he couldn't slam on the brakes fast enough. Jill screamed while she watched in horror as the car slammed into her mother knocking her over the hood. Her body crashed into the windshield and became wedged there.

The car came to a screeching stop.

Jill ran to her mother.

The driver of the car was already calling for help. He happened to be an off-duty police officer who was driving his personal car. He used his police radio to call for an ambulance.

Jill said that everything was a blur from then on. Helpful and curious people began to gather and some of them pulled her away from the scene. The ambulance arrived and the paramedics carefully removed her mother from the wrecked car and took her to the hospital. A kind couple gave Jill a ride to the hospital where she went to the Intensive Care Unit. She was satisfied that a medical team was doing everything they could for her mother and then she thought to call me. She called our home and Mary told her where I was. An operator helped Jill locate the number of the church in Gettysburg and put the call through for her.

The funeral was held four weeks before Christmas. People in the rural community turn out in large numbers for funerals because everyone is either related or well acquainted and they want to show their love and concern. The church was especially crowded for the funeral of a young mother, who was deeply loved by the community, and who died such a tragic death at a time when everyone should be happy. It was a difficult funeral to prepare for. I struggled with trying to make sense out of this tragedy for the family. I finally gave up on that and simply entrusted Helen into the loving arms of her Savior in heaven. I encouraged the family to hold on to God's promise that he knows what's best for them and for Helen. After all, their mother was celebrating her greatest Christmas with her newborn King in heaven. I ached to give them more but that is the best there is.

It wasn't much of a joyous Christmas for Helen's family. They missed her terribly and that's understandable.

Chapter 14 - The Wedding My Dog Attended

"There is a time for everything and a season for every activity under heaven." Proverbs 3:1

I have heard pastors say, "I would rather do ten funerals than one wedding." The reason was that everyone involved in a wedding is usually nervous, uptight and concerned that everything will be just perfect. If things aren't going well, it's very easy to blame the pastor just because he's handy. On the other hand, at a funeral people are looking to be consoled and comforted. Any words of consolation the pastor might say are usually well received and make him the hero of the day.

This was one of those fun weddings where everyone seemed relaxed.

The story began the day I was installed as pastor of Peace Lutheran Church in Rapid City, South Dakota. A good-looking young couple with love in their eyes and smiling faces came up to me with a sheepish look. They had set the date of their wedding for later that month in anticipation of my arrival. They were hoping that my calendar would permit me to perform the ceremony. The young couple seemed mature and very much in love just as you would picture the ideal wedding couple. I checked my schedule and told them that I would be happy to perform their wedding.

The day of the wedding arrived. It was very warm, there was hardly a breeze stirring and all of the doors and windows of the church were open to try and keep things as cool as possible. I was informed at the rehearsal that it was traditional for the groom and his groomsmen to get dressed in the parsonage basement. It was a handy location across the alley from the church.

Everything was progressing like a well-oiled machine until minutes before the ceremony. After dressing in his handsome white tuxedo the groom arrived at the church, checked his pocket and discovered that he was missing the wedding ring for his bride. He remembered that it must be back at the pastor's house and sent one of his groomsmen back to get it. In his haste to get back to the church after fetching the ring, the groomsman forgot to close the gate to our yard.

This allowed our terrier, Skippy, to roam more freely than he was normally permitted.

Skippy was a friendly dog that never met a person he didn't like. He was mostly white with black spots. One of the black spots encircled an eye and made him look like half a bandit. He had short legs and only stood about a foot high.

The wedding began in fine style. The bride was radiant and beautiful and the groom was handsome and tall as they stood before me. As I delivered the wedding message on that warm and exceedingly humid June day, I noticed that the groom was sweating profusely. In fact the sweat was dripping down his forehead and off of the tip of his nose. It looked very uncomfortable. I finished the message and pulled the handkerchief out of my pocket and handed it to him as the soloist began to sing.

I expected him to wipe his face with it, but he blew his nose in it and handed it back to me.

As I tucked the handkerchief back into my pocket something attracted my attention. Out of the corner of my eye I noticed something white with black spots prancing toward the front of the church. I shot a quick glance in that direction and realized that it was Skippy. He had made his way down the side aisle and was exploring uncharted areas. He hadn't seen me yet, but was checking out the bridesmaids' dresses by sniffing them one at a time.

I was afraid that he might lift his leg and baptize a chosen dress.

But Skippy moved on, walking across the bride's train. That's when he looked up and our eyes met. He wagged his tail in recognition and I was sure he was going to bound up the steps to greet me. Not wanting this to happen, I muttered under my breath hoping the dog could hear or read my lips, "Don't you come up here!"

The bride thought I was talking to her and asked, "What did you say?"

"I'm not talking to you!" I whispered.

All this time the soloist was singing and the bride and groom didn't know that Skippy was behind them. The bride looked at the groom with some alarm and wondered if I had lost my senses.

I needed to gain control of this situation quickly before it got out of hand if it wasn't already. There was a little room to the left of the altar area and I thought, *if I could get Skippy in there the matter would be resolved at least until after the wedding.* Realizing that the soloist would sing for a while longer, I left the bridal couple and went to a door on my left that led to the small storeroom. Another door from that room opened toward the congregation only a few feet away from were the groom's parents were sitting. I called out in a whisper, "Skippy, come here!"

From my vantage point, I couldn't see the dog and I didn't get any response. I wished the soloist would sing a little louder to cover up my dog calling.

I received no help from her, for as she sang from the back balcony of the church, she was oblivious to what was happening in front. I tried calling Skippy again with no results. It was obvious that the soloist was coming to the end of the song, so I had to get back to the bride and groom. I moved back to the door facing the altar area and opened it a crack. I could see the bridal couple and they could see my eye peeking out. They looked relieved. They told me later that they thought the heat got to me and that I went into that room and passed out.

I waited until the soloist was about finished singing before I nonchalantly returned to my place before the bride and groom. I couldn't see Skippy anywhere. A bit puzzled but yet determined to finish the ceremony as if nothing out of the ordinary happened, I carried on till the end of the service.

Following the ceremony I conferred with Mary about what had happened to Skippy and she filled me in on the rest of the story.

Mary had been sitting toward the back of the church near the middle aisle with our daughter, Lisa, sitting on her lap. She told me that while I was in the little storeroom, Skippy lost interest in what was going on and decided to walk down the center aisle on the white runner. Lisa spotted him coming down the aisle and announced to her mother, "There's Skippy!"

Mary thought, it couldn't be--- and yet it was!

There was Skippy prancing down the center aisle on the white runner just as proud as he could be with the wedding guests gesturing him toward the back of the church. Mary picked up Skippy and carried him to the back of the church. As she did this, the photographer took a flash picture of her and Skippy. Evidently he thought this would be a great picture to capture as a memento for the bridal couple. It mustn't have turn out because we never saw the picture. Mary returned Skippy to the sanctuary of our back yard and he was happy to be back in his familiar surroundings, none the wiser of the stir he caused.

I was quite concerned about how the bride's mother would react to the sideshow at her daughter's wedding because she seemed to be the type of person who liked things to go just right. I went to her as soon as I could to apologize for my dog's attendance at the wedding without an invitation and to explain how he got there.

My fears were unfounded. She dismissed the situation with a big grin and said, “That’s all right, Pastor, we’ll just put into our thank you notes that everyone and their dog came to the wedding.”

After that experience I believed that nothing much worse could happen at one of my weddings, so I tried to relax.

Boy, was I wrong!

Peace Lutheran Church in Rapid City

Chapter 15 – The Bride in the Bib Overalls and the Reluctant Groom

"A time to be silent and a time to speak." Proverbs 3:7

A pastor friend of mine told me that the hardest lesson he learned about the ministry was that you could not please everyone. I had the feeling it was going to be one of those situations as I spoke to the lady on the phone.

She called about 9:00 A.M. on Saturday morning, which was my day off. The purpose of her call was to find out if I would officiate at her wedding, which she wanted that afternoon.

Her story, and I mean story, was that she had spoken to a neighboring pastor about getting married and he referred her to me because he would be out of town at a conference. The rest of her story was so confusing that I agreed to meet with her at 10:00 A.M. at the church to try to sort things out and to talk about the possibility of the wedding that day.

In the mean time I telephoned the referring pastor. His wife answered the phone. She filled me in, " The lady called me this morning around 8:30. She wanted my husband to have her wedding this afternoon. I told her it was out of the question because Harold was out of town at a church conference. She abruptly hung up on me. I certainly didn't suggest she call you." I don't appreciate people who lie. This gal was not starting out on solid ground with me at all but I was curious.

The couple arrived 15 minutes late for their appointment, which left another negative impression on me. I heard the door of the church opening so I went out into the hall to direct the couple to my office. What greeted my eyes shocked and embarrassed me.

I was greeted with the vision of a brassy looking woman in her late 20's with a very determined look on her face. She had short blond hair cropped around eyes that immediately said to me, "Don't cross me!" She wore no makeup and had a stride like a locomotive. She was pretty in a coarse sort of way and wore bib overalls like train engineers wore in the 50' and 60's.

What hit me like a ton of bricks was that the bib part was cut down the front about 6 inches with about a 2-inch gape and I mean, **gape**. It would have been appropriate if she was wearing some sort of top but, she wore no blouse or bra, which, you can imagine, revealed quite a lot for she was... well...she was very well endowed.

The words of a 1940's song came to mind, "June is busting out all over." But I didn't dare sing. They were definitely weapons of mass distraction.

I was feeling very uncomfortable about being alone with this woman, so I asked her, "Where's the groom?"

"He's in the parking lot by the car and won't come in."

Now this was my first hint that he was a reluctant groom.

I was concerned about being alone in the church with this woman who flaunted what she had, so I pointed out my office as I headed out to the parking lot to get him.

I found him leaning against his pickup truck with one foot on the ground and the other propped against the running board. His arms were folded across his chest as if to say, "I'm not in agreement with what's happening here." He was tall, dark and handsome and looked like a good catch for some woman. He had a kind face that reflected the fear of a trapped animal but there was sincerity about him that I could see through his fear. With some coaxing the young man came with me into my office where the woman waited impatiently. The expression on his face made me feel like I had just invited him to his own execution.

After many prying questions the story took a warped shape.

The couple had been living together for some time. The gal in the bib overalls was tired of waiting for a proposal and tricked the young man into agreeing to get married. He was thinking sometime in the future when she said, "Let's do it today!"

Now he was trapped.

She put the wheels in motion so that he couldn't wiggle out of his promise. She immediately called the groom's pastor, who was out of town. She said that the pastor's wife told her that if they wanted to get married that day, they might call Pastor Grassinger. I knew that was a lie.

The young man felt like he was in over his head. He agreed to the marriage to shut her up. Now she was calling his bluff by wanting to get married that day. I could tell immediately that he felt that he had fallen into a deep hole and couldn't get out.

As we visited, I asked them if they understood that they were living together in sin in the eyes of the Lord. The gal said, "No, where does it say that?"

I countered with, "Do you know what the sixth commandment says?" I directed my question to the perspective groom because he was the Lutheran.

"The sixth commandment? Uh, no. What is it?"

"Thou shalt not commit adultery!"

Then the gal piped up and said, "Who cares about the commandments any way, they're out of date!"

Now if you want to say something to agitate a Bible based, Lutheran minister, those are fighting words.

You could feel the tension increasing in my office. I felt like I was riding on a runaway train that was speeding out of control. Somehow, I had to apply the brakes. Trying to keep my gaze from the top of her overalls, I asked, "If you don't care about keeping God's commandments, why are you here asking for Christ's blessing upon your marriage?"

"Where else can we go to get married on short notice?"

Now I was quite tense, so I shot back, "You could go to a justice of the peace or find a ship's captain!"

"There are no captains in Rapid City and you can't find a justice of the peace on Saturday," she snapped back at me.

"So the reason you called me today is that I am the only one available to perform your marriage and you don't care if God is a part of it or not!" I challenged.

"I don't care about the commandments and I don't care about God. All I want to do is get married today!"

The young man was now sitting on the edge of his chair obviously enjoying the little repartee. He even had a little smirk on his face that communicated to me, "Go get her pastor!"

Quite annoyed by now, I replied in a definite tone, "If you don't care about God or His commandments then I don't care to perform your wedding!"

Now the gal was quite agitated and she rose from her chair and headed for the door. "Fine!" she growled back, "I don't want you to perform our wedding either!"

She stomped out.

The man and I were left looking at each other and I wondered how he would react.

It wasn't long in coming.

He got up with a big grin on his face and without saying a word gave me the okay sign with his fingers and followed his "finance" out.

Usually following an encounter like this I would feel shaken and uneasy, but this time I didn't. The words, "you can't please everyone" echoed in my mind and I was grateful for my friend's wise counsel. Actually I felt great relief from being spared from having to perform this wedding. I knew the groom was relieved too, at least for the time being.

Chapter 16 – The Devastating Flood of 1972

"Therefore everyone who hears these words of mine and puts them into practice is like a wise man that built his house on a rock. The rain came down, the streams rose, and the winds blew and beat against that house; yet it did not fall, because it had its foundation on the rock." St. Matthew 7:24-25

Sometimes following the most peaceful situations, God can bring turmoil and devastation and we wonder what lesson he is trying to teach us. I have learned that patience is a virtue and sooner or later God will make clear a very important lesson. Our difficult job is to be patient until he does.

It was 1972 the year a rain storm and ensuing flood devastated Keystone in the Black Hills and ripped through the middle of Rapid City leaving 238 people dead.

The week didn't start out to be tragic. It was June, and the children were happy to be out of school. Peace Lutheran Church was holding its annual Vacation Bible School. About 75 eager children had gathered to learn about the workings of God's creation through nature and how they might help take care of the world he created for us.

Little did I realize as the week began that God had his own dramatic lesson about nature to teach us.

The week of June 4th began with beautiful spring weather when everything is budding into new life. The fresh sap rising in the pine trees nearby in the Black Hills gave a delightfully fragrant smell as the gentile breeze wafted it into town. Added to this therapeutic aroma were the sights and sounds of excited voices of children eager to learn more about God's love for them. We lived in an ideal location to learn about how God provides for us through the beauties of His world because they are so obvious in the Black Hills area. Mary and I organized the VBS that year and we were surrounded with an excellent staff of teachers and helpers. We taught songs and read scripture passages that applied to God's wonderful creation, all the while applying the truths of the ecological lessons.

As the week progressed, it was obvious to everyone that the temperature was climbing and so was the humidity. By Thursday it was not only the temperature that was rising, but also the tempers of the children. Patience was replaced with little skirmishes of frustration. Looking back, if we had been perceptive enough to interpret the native signs of the restless children, we might have issued a warning.

But we didn't have a clue.

Friday morning dawned with the highest humidity of the week. Black, ominous clouds seemed to be stuck like a dark gray cap perched on top of the Black Hills. It appeared that we were in for a downpour later in the day, but the clouds didn't budge and weather reports were telling us that they were dumping lots of rain in the Hills.

VBS ended at noon and the children were sent home with instructions to bring their parents and friends to an evening program. The teachers stayed for a while to make sure that everything was ready to display the children's projects to demonstrate what they had learned during the week.

The time came and the church was full of proud parents eager to see their children sing or recite a verse and to see what they had made.

It was while we were in church that an ominous and early darkness fell. Lightening flashed outside and thunder shook the church. The pitter-patter of rain started slowly at first but soon grew into sheets blown by the wind.

The program in the church ended and there was a mad dash through the rain to the Parish Hall, which was about 40 yards from the church. A rich fare of coffee, cookies and lemon aid was set up for socialization and relaxation. But there was something about the weather that was not allowing anyone to relax. So people sipped their beverage, politely ate a cookie or two and headed for their cars and home.

The first clue that something ominous was taking place was when Harold Gamble rushed in from the rain, found his wife in the kitchen, spoke to her in a hushed voice, hustled her and his children into their waiting car and disappeared into the darkness and rain. He was overheard telling his wife, "We can't go back home! The creek is rising fast and our home is in danger!"

Other ladies finished the clean up and we locked up the Parish Hall for the night and returned to our parsonage next door.

The relentless rain was coming down by the buckets.

Without any inkling of the magnitude of what was taking place around us, we got our three young children Lisa, Lori and Scott off to bed. Our plan was to drop them off at the home of some members and good friends, Jack and Lena early the next morning. Then Mary and I would attend the state convention of The

Lutheran Laymen's League that was meeting in Sioux Falls that weekend.

As we settled into bed, we listened to the radio reports of flooding in the Hills. We were startled by a bolt of lightening that struck so close that it was like a flash camera going off in our bedroom. The flash was followed immediately by the thunder that shook the house. Then the electricity went out and the radio went dead.

Now the only thing to do was try and go to sleep. But that didn't last long. We heard some strange noises outside our bedroom window. They came from the house next door. The sounds were bang! Bang! Bang! Bang! Swoosh! And then we could hear water running.

I jumped out of bed to look out the window. At first couldn't see anything in the darkness. As I strained to see what was going on, a flash of lightening revealed the silhouette of our neighbor, Mr. Muffin, with a pail in his hand. A succession of lightening strikes that appeared like the slow but deliberate snap shots in a strobe light revealed that Mr. Muffin was feverishly bailing out his basement and dumping the water out his side door.

What bothered me about this procedure was that he was not paying attention to where he was throwing his bailed water, which was right at our basement that was prone to have a water problem of its own.

My wife still laughs at the scene that followed. Dressed only in my pajamas, I went out the back door and hugged the house to be somewhat protected from the pouring rain. I sloshed to the corner of the house where I was hidden from Mr. Muffin by the bushes and waited for him to come to his door with the next pail full of water. "Mr. Muffin!" I said in a pleading voice, "Would you be so kind as to dump your water toward the back of your house? It's running into our basement!" Startled by the voice out of the darkness and rain, Mr. Muffin who was breathing hard, replied between puffs, "Oh sure! (Puff) I didn't realize (puff) that it was running (puff) toward your house. (Puff) Sorry!"

By the time I returned to the house satisfied that Mr. Muffin was bailing in an approved way, I was completely soaked and looked like a drowned preacher. There was nothing left to do but to dry off, ignore the storm and the regular sound of Mr. Muffin's bailing and go back to bed.

The next thing I knew, the ringing of the telephone was jarring me awake. The first rays of the morning sun reassured me that the rain was over and I reached for the complaining phone.

"There's been a big flood! Don't drink the water! Keystone has been wiped out!" It was the excited voice of Pastor Marty, a retired pastor in our congregation. He filled me in on what had happed over night reciting it like a street corner newsboy shouting the headlines. "The floodwaters washed through Rapid City and left lots of destruction in its wake. The water plant was inundated and the supply was tainted so don't drink the water. Turn on your radio and you'll get the full report!"

We obediently turned on the radio and the full extent of the storm's destruction unfolded. The menacing black clouds we saw camped over the Hills dumped 15 inches of rain on two peaks. The resulting deluge rushed down the mountainside into the valley and then into Rapid Creek. This sent a total of 30 inches of frothing, exploding water that spouted through the Black Hills destroying everything in its path.

Rapid Valley narrows just before it enters the city and it compressed the millions of gallons of cascading water from the creek as though it was being forced through a funnel. It resulted in the water being given the force of a speeding locomotive at full throttle.

During the night Bill Fisher, a ranger with the South Dakota Department of Fish and Wildlife, was called out to go up into the Hills and warn those living or camping along the creek of the impending danger and to tell them to evacuate immediately. He lived with his wife and twin boys in a home on the fish hatchery property that was located where the creek enters Rapid City directly below the valley. Around 9:30 that night he called his wife and told her to grab the boys, get them into the car without delay and drive to his mother's place, which was on high ground.

But Lois didn't grasp the urgency of Bill's plea and paused to gather a few items that were precious to the family. She also tarried in the hope that Bill would return to go with them. She was just getting into the car with the boys when the full force of the water hit. The power of that water took the car, the family and the house and washed it all down the creek. Nothing identifiable of the house was ever found only the concrete pad on which it sat was left. The car was later discovered and it was a heap of twisted rubble wrapped around a tree. No one was inside.

Lois and the boys were missing.

After destroying the house, the water poured into the picturesque Canyon Lake Park at an alarming rate. A small earthen dam attempted to valiantly hold back the pouring water as long as it could. But soon, water violently rushed over the berm in the blackness of the powerless night until finally the dam gave way.

Suddenly the foaming water that had been washing over the dam was augmented with the powerful force of a wall of water over ten feet high rushing full tilt into the residential part of Rapid City.

Mark and Carrie Boyle had been married just three weeks. At the young age of 17 and 18 with no job, they were living in the basement of the Boyle family home. Something awakened Mark during that stormy night. He wasn't quite sure what it was. Maybe it was the sound of gurgling water coming from the basement drain. For some strange reason he was drawn to get out of bed and peer out of the basement window.

What he saw sent a chill through his body that he will never forget.

He watched as a ten-foot wall of water crashed toward the house. He watched in horror as the force of that wall of water picked up a Buick sedan that was parked at the curb, tossed it into the air and swallowed it before his eyes.

Realizing that he didn't have a split second to waste even to wake his pregnant new bride and explain what was happening, he grabbed her wrist and instantly began to drag her up the basement steps. Carrie protested loudly in her sleepy state, "Mark, what are you doing? Let me sleep!"

As the couple reached the first step they heard the window braking behind them. Carrie cried out, "What's happening?" Mark tried to explain as he continued half dragging her up the stairs.

"Flood! Wall of water! Ten feet! Swallowed a car! Got to get out!" Mark shouted over the deafening noise of the rushing water.

Carrie got her feet under her on the middle step and she looked back in disbelief as she saw the rushing water pouring into the basement.

It was chasing them up the steps.

Once upstairs, they realized they were still in great danger and Mark had to wake his parents and get them to the second floor. "No time to explain! Get up! We have to get upstairs! There's a flood! Come on! Let's go!"

When they got to the second floor, the family looked out of the window in shock and bewilderment. There was a lake of water around them that had never been there before and it was rising fast.

"What do we do now?" said Mark's Dad.

"We wait and pray that the force of the water doesn't wash the house off the foundation," answered Mark.

As they were considering other options, they heard the voices of children screaming for help. Peering out the window, they could see four children between the ages of six and twelve looking back at them from the upstairs window of the house next door. There were no adults with them.

The children's eyes were as big as silver dollars and were filled with fright. After opening the windows they were able to shout back and forth over the blast of the storm and the roar of the rushing water.

"Just try to stay calm" Lenny called to them. "We'll try to figure out how to help you." The oldest girl yelled, back, "Please hurry! The house is shaking and I'm afraid it is going to fall apart."

At just that moment the house the children were in came free from its foundation and began to float toward the Boyle home. Midst the screams of the children and the panic of the Boyle's, God, being the loving Lord He is, guided that floating house so that the two windows through which they were communicating lined up perfectly. There was an old twin mattress upstairs, which Mark and his dad laid from window to window so that the children could scramble to the safety of the Boyle home. The two families huddled in the house that held securely until the floodwaters subsided several hours later.

Meanwhile, that wall of water continued through town destroying a children's park called Story Book Island. The park was filled with statues of famous characters depicting scenes from children's stories like Cinderella and Sleeping Beauty.

Sometimes there is humor in the midst of great tragedy. The morning after the flood, Cinderella's life size pumpkin carriage had washed up in front of a shoe store in nearby Bakken Park shopping center. If one didn't know better, it appeared as if Cinderella had stopped by to replace her lost glass slipper.

The automobile dealership in the flood's path didn't stand a chance. Cars were strewn everywhere, crumpled in heaps where they came to rest in every position some hundreds of yards from where they had been parked. One car came to rest leaning against a telephone pole at a 45-degree angle. It looked like a phantom driver had taken a run at the pole and driven up as far as he could and left it there.

A half-mile swath of destruction wound its way along the path of Rapid Creek, destroying expensive homes in the Canyon Lake area. The parking lot of Central High School was washed clean and stripped of any cars left over night. The school itself was weakened so that, to the delight of students, classes had to be cancelled until temporary repairs could be made.

Through the center of town many old and run down homes were either flattened or made uninhabitable. Reconstruction efforts turned that flood plane into a beautiful park area that followed the meanderings of Rapid Creek. The park was a definite improvement over the former blighted area.

Needless to say, Mary and I did not go to the Lutheran Laymen's convention. The home of the couple where our children were to stay was only feet from where the floodwaters stopped. It was not a time to be away from our children and our members and neighbors in the flood area needed assistance. In the days following the flood, I helped distribute drinking water at a nearby fire station.

Only emergency and construction vehicles were permitted to drive around Rapid City because of the devastation and out of concern for looting. I found a clergy sign that I had in the car, placed it in the window and was given access to where ever I wanted to go.

I checked on various members that I knew lived in the flood plain. I went to the home of a sweet couple who were well into their eighty's named Martha and Eddie. They lived just a Catholic Church plus two houses away from Rapid Creek. I could see that the Catholic Church, which was significantly down hill from Martha and Eddie's house had been deeply engulfed in water. I learned later that a beloved priest had drowned in the basement.

Martha and Eddie weren't at home, but I could see that water had risen well above the six steps one had to climb to get to their front door. There were watermarks about 5 feet up on the main level on which they lived.

A neighbor who lived between the church and the couple's home was raking up debris. I walked over to ask him if he had seen Martha and Eddie. "No," he said "but I heard they had gotten out safely and were staying with their son."

I was anxious to find out what happened to them and to hear how they got out of their home safely. So I drove up to their son's place that was high and away from the creek.

Martha and Eddie took turns telling me the most amazing story of how God takes care of His children and provides miraculous circumstances and perfect timing to accomplish His purposes. They had been fast asleep during the storm, unaware of their danger. Martha told me that she awoke with a start, but needed to use the bathroom. When she put her feet on the floor the little throw rug by the bed was wet. But nature called in an urgent way and needed to be tended to before anything else. As she walked into the bathroom she was standing in water that was now ankle deep. She automatically turned on light switch, but nothing happened.

Thank the Lord the power was off or she would have been electrocuted!

She felt around in the darkness and managed to accomplish what she needed to do while, all the time, wondering where the water was coming from.

It was getting deeper.

By the time she got back to the bed where Eddie lay, the water was just below the top of the mattress. Eddie always kept a flashlight in the stand by the bed. Martha reached for it as she awakened Eddie. She turned it on and amazingly it worked. She helped Eddie get out of bed while she shinned the flashlight around the bedroom, Martha knew they needed to get out of the house immediately. "Eddie!" Martha cried out. "The creek must be flooding and the water is rising fast! We need to get out of here!"

Following the beam of the flashlight, they found their way to the front door and onto the front porch. The rushing water pushed against their bodies and they held on to each other to keep their balance. If they lost their footing they would be washed away. They wrapped themselves around a column that supported their porch roof and hung on for dear life. Martha panned the flashlight around to survey the situation. What they saw caused their hearts to sink. There was rushing water everywhere as far as the beam of the flashlight could reach.

They felt there was no hope!

This was it!

They would die together in the floodwater.

They realized that, in descending the six steps to the ground, they would be in water several feet above their heads. Neither of them could swim or, even if they could, would have the stamina to make it against the rushing current. Martha continued beaming the flashlight around to see if they had any options while Eddie prayed.

There were none.

But as God guides all things, his timing was perfect. At exactly the same time that Martha's flashlight beamed at the concrete of the highway that was above their street, a military truck of National Guard troops was going by. They saw the flashlight and instantly recognized the danger of the couple below and stopped to put their evacuation training into practice. Two of the guardsmen tied ropes around their waists and jumped from the highway above and swam to Martha and Eddie's rescue. The couple clung to the guardsmen with all the strength they had while those above pulled them against the swift current to the safety of the waiting truck. The guardsmen wrapped them in blankets to keep them warm and whisked them off to their son's home where they were grateful to be safe and high and dry.

If that wasn't a miraculous rescue timed to perfection, then I don't know what is.

Our remaining church members that lived in the flood plains had either evacuated safely or were not in danger. One lady had to sit on her kitchen counter until the water went down. She was a little shaken, but survived.

As the days after the flood passed, many stories mingling tragedy and humor were told.

The Rapid City Journal published a story that reported the results of a sweeping search of the flood area by National Guard Troops. The morning after the flood several troops were surprised to discover a modest home that had been wrenched from its foundation and had floated onto the neighboring golf course. The house was completely intact and sat there as if it belonged, only without a foundation.

Following their orders, the Guard Troops knocked on the door and got no response. So they broke it open and began a check of the rooms for bodies. One of the men opened the door to the bedroom and was surprised to find an elderly husband and wife still sound asleep in the tiny room. The guardsman called his buddy to come see what he found and then attempted to gently awaken the sleeping couple. But how do two National Guard troops wake someone gently in this kind of situation?

The couple was quite alarmed to open their eyes and find two men in uniform standing over them. One can imagine what thoughts must have gone through their minds. The woman screamed and the man didn't know whether to defend himself from intruders or if the angels that transport people to heaven wore military fatigues.

Rather than to try and explain, the guardsman told the husband to get out of bed, look out the window and see where they were. "How in the world did we get here?" asked the elderly man as he looked out the window in disbelief.

After the couple calmed down and the guardsmen were able to relate about the flood that took place during the night, the husband explained in a loud voice, "We are both very hard of hearing and when we take out our hearing aids at night, we don't hear anything. But there is an advantage, we sleep very soundly."

The Harold Gamble family was in church the Sunday following the flood. Harold told me that that hey spent the night in a motel. The next day they drove to see what damage the flood had done to their home. During the night the water began to wash their home off of its foundation and their propane tank exploded. The only identifiable part of their home was the roof that had blown off and ended up in the trees beside the creek. Harold, who had recently joined our church with his family, still gave thanks to God in the midst of their loss. He confessed to me, "We lost just about everything we own but God spared our family and I am grateful that we are still together. With God's blessings we will rebuild but not back next to the creek."

Members of our church turned out to assist them in the recovery of a very few precious belongings and provided them with food and clothing until they could get on their feet. Mary and I took the family into our home until they could find appropriate temporary housing.

The Sunday following the flood I received the call for pastors to volunteer for ministry to families trying to identify the bodies of loved ones.

I answered the call.

After completing the Sunday service at church, which was packed because people felt they better listen to what God was trying to tell them by means of the flood, I went to the closer of the two funeral homes in town. There was a five-minute orientation and training session before I was thrown into the thick of things. Armed only with prayer and a desire to comfort and help those who eagerly sought to identify their loved ones, but also were afraid of finding them, I moved over to a husband and wife in their middle forties. They were a nice looking couple dressed in casual clothes. There was an air of dignity and pride about them, but great hurt and fear filled their faces. They were holding hands and the knuckles of the husband were white as they clasped hands.

I introduced myself and explained why I had come over to them. I spoke to them in a comforting tone of voice as I attempted to ease their apprehension by demonstrating that I was there for the purpose of helping and comforting them. I asked them whom they were searching for and they poured out their story.

They explained that they were looking for their 23-year-old daughter who had gone out with her boyfriend Friday evening. The couple had gone to a bar in the general area of Rapid Creek. They related the story from the boyfriend's point of view because he survived the flood but their daughter was missing. He told the parents that they had a few drinks with friends and he was getting nervous about the downpour outside and realized their proximity to the creek might put them in danger. He wanted to leave but she was enjoying her visit with friends and wanted to stay. There was a disagreement between them with a few harsh words and he decided to go home but she was going to stay and come home later with her friends.

That was the last anyone saw her.

I sensed that the parents were peeved at the boyfriend because he survived and their daughter was missing. They told me that they were disappointed that he did not take better care of their daughter by convincing her to leave when he did. If he had, she would still be alive. They had already searched for their daughter at the Catron Funeral Home that was across town, where they found a woman that appeared to be about their daughter's age, weight and height. However, they were unable to make a positive identification because the girl's face was battered beyond recognition and her hair was darker than their daughter's. They were here now, because they wanted to see if they could locate a body that more closely resembled their daughter. It was obvious that they were hoping to find some comfort, no matter how small, in locating a body that had not suffered as much trauma.

I offered to pray with them before we began our search. The husband and wife were still gripping hands as we bowed our heads. "Father," I prayed. "Give this couple strength and courage as we search for their daughter. Grant them keen eyes to see through the ravages of the storm to identify their beloved daughter. And when they find her, lift them up by your loving and gracious spirit and help them to accept the truth that she is with you in the glory and peace of heaven. Help them, Lord, to have comfort in the fact that she is not suffering any pain or sadness as she rests in your loving arms. Reassure them that they will one day be reunited with her forever in the glory of heaven. Amen."

With great apprehension we walked together into the extremely large garage of the funeral home. It was a typically cold garage with a concrete floor. There was nothing ceremonial about it. Its rectangular shape could hold a double row of hearses, limousines or funeral cars that stretched four deep.

The garage had been emptied of cars and in their place were rows and rows of bodies that had been stripped of their clothes, hastily rinsed with a hose and unceremoniously laid on the floor covered with sheets. Only the corpses heads and feet were exposed for identification purposes. The bodies were grouped in categories of old, middle age and young men and women and boys and girls of various ages. Red tags were attached to the toe of one body in each category to guide the bereaved loved ones through the maze of bodies.

The workers preparing the bodies for display had to become detached from their task or they would crumble in despair. Ravaged by hunger they occasionally took a quick break from their morbid activity to grab a bite of sandwich and wash it down with some coffee. I wondered how they could eat anything in the midst of such stench and death. How sanitary could it be to eat with unwashed hands that had been in contact with bodies that had been decaying for 36 hours?

The parents walked slowly down the rows of the dead. When they located the section appropriate to their daughter's description, they painfully scanned each face searching for recognition.

They found none.

Occasionally their gaze would pan across the rows and rows of bodies with heartfelt compassion for other families who had lost their loved ones and to make sure they did not miss anyone that might be their daughter.

Downcast, they shrugged their shoulders and decided to return to the other funeral home to take a second look at the body that most closely resembled their daughter. They thanked me and promised to call and let me know the results of their continued search.

That evening I received a phone call from the father informing me that they had identified their daughter's body at Catron Funeral Home. It was the person they had looked at before, but they didn't want to admit it to themselves because her disfigured face gave evidence of what she suffered before her death. He thanked me again for my comfort, the prayer and helping them to focus on the truth that their daughter was in heaven.

Bill Fisher searched the two funeral homes for the bodies of his wife and twin boys with a devastated heart. I don't know why, but he had in mind that he would discover his wife first. But while searching for her, he unexpectedly came upon the bodies of his boys. He lost his composure so completely that he overlooked his wife lying nearby. Bill was never the same person after that.

Several days later Mary and I were visiting at the home of our good friends and neighbors Carolyn and Merle. They shared an account told to them by a friend named, Don, who belonged to their square dance club. He was in shock as he related that he and his wife, Doris, had been camping in the Black Hills with some friends the night of the storm. Campers considered the choice sites to be close to Rapid Creek and they were enjoying two such campsites with some close friends. A steady, heavy rain started coming down, but there was nothing to suggest any danger until a park ranger drove through the campground warning the campers of the approaching flood and ordering them to move to higher ground.

The two couples began to break camp immediately but it was not long before the creek began to rise fast. Both husbands ordered their wives to climb to higher ground while they stayed behind to hook up their campers. The other husband broke camp and drove out first just making it to higher ground. But, as Don was attempting to drive off, the flood hit and carried his SUV and camper with it. The force of the floodwater carried his vehicle several 100 yards down stream bouncing it around like a toy car. He thought he was gone for sure until the SUV miraculously gained traction on a hill, which led to a road heading up and out of the valley. He drove to safety leaving the rig on high ground and doubled back on foot to retrieve Doris. He searched every inch of that hill where he sent her. He scoured it over and over again for over an hour calling out his wife's name in the pitch darkness with the sound of the roaring water still rushing below. Only an empty echo answered his furtive call. Everyone else had left the area.

He had lost her!

He had also lost contact with his friends.

Finally he had no choice but to return home alone.

The day following the flood, he was able to connect with his camping friends. He rejoiced that both husband and wife had made it to safety. It was the wife who told him that she and Doris obediently climbed to the safety of the nearby hill. Then she told the horrifying story of how Doris saw that Don was ready to drive away and, not wanting to be left behind, rushed down the hill to the SUV and banged at the passenger side door screaming at him to stop and let her in. The woman continued her account of what happened in a somber tone of voice telling how Doris yelled at him as he started to pull away but her screams were lost in the roar of the floodwater. That's when the flood hit the SUV and camper sweeping it and Doris away. That's the last she saw her.

He hadn't heard her screams!

He had no idea that she was there!

They had been so close to getting out together.

But it was not to be.

"Why?" he asked.

Don was devastated at loosing his life partner!

Two weeks later a local television station reported that two teenage boys who were out for a hike, smelled something foul. They reported it to the authorities and a search of the area was made. A badly decomposed body of a middle age female was found wedged high in the branches of a tree.

Clothing revealed that it was Doris.

It is impossible to understand the destructive force of water descending at breakneck speed unless you have lived through it. Equally impossible to comprehend is the tremendous grief of losing a loved one in such a tragedy. The experience of having the one you love beside you in great contentment one moment then suddenly vanished from you forever, is beyond comprehension. Our human attempts to answer the searching question of "Why?" fail miserably. At these times, there is no substitute for total trust in a comforting and loving God. Our God is one who understands our weaknesses and reaches out to those who turn to Him with the promise of his love and grants us the reassurance that the one they love is safe in His almighty arms in heaven. This is the comforting lesson God teaches us even in devastation and loss.

A minister of the Gospel of our Lord, Jesus Christ, is armed with the gift of applying God's joyous promises to all who are hurting. The gift must never be withheld. It is the greatest gift anyone can give!

Carrie and Mark Boyle after the flood.

Chapter 17 – You Know da Governor?

"You are looking only on the surface of things." II Corinthians 10:7

A willingness to serve in extra capacities in a pastoral role may have its perks. It may be loads of fun, but also lots of work. However, when all is considered, there can be many blessings as one volunteers to serve the Lord in a variety of valuable ministries.

I served as Pastoral Advisor for The South Dakota District of The Lutheran Layman's League from 1971 through 1974. During that time, Mary and I attended International L.L.L. Conventions in Miami, San Francisco, Washington D.C. and St. Louis. Although each convention was enjoyable and a learning experience, the convention in San Francisco took a strange turn.

Mary and I were excited about flying into San Francisco for the convention and meeting friends that we had not seen since the year before in Miami. It was there that we met and formed a close friendship with some L.L.L.ers from Minnesota named Sal and Jen.

We landed at the airport in San Francisco and were whisked off to the hotel by cab. I wondered if the location of the convention hotel in the red light district of the downtown area was a colossal mistake or a brilliant opportunity for Christian witnessing. For, as we pulled up in front of the hotel, it was obvious by the signs advertising "Top and Bottomless Strip Clubs" that we were in uncharted waters—at least for us. As others from the sheltered Midwest pulled up in front of the hotel many commented, "Let's go back home!"

From our hotel room window on the 9th floor we could see a large billboard plastered on the building across the street advertising "The Lutheran Hour" with a gigantic picture of the much loved and respected speaker, Dr. Oswald Hoffmann. At first we were impressed that the convention planning committee had done such a thorough job of getting a wonderful sign advertising The Lutheran Hour outside the convention hotel. Then we continued our gaze down the side of the building to the ad that was painted underneath. Appearing to continuing from the words on the billboard "Tune into The Lutheran Hour and hear Dr. Oswald Hoffmann" one could read, "All night top and bottomless clubs. We invite you to see it all." I knew this wasn't Dr. Hoffmann's intended message at all.

As the convention progressed, stories circulated about Lutheran laymen who were propositioned by prostitutes as they walked the streets near the hotel. These Christian laymen had the opportunity to witness to their faith in Jesus as a loving and forgiving Savior from sin and to tell these young women that Jesus died on the cross also to forgive their sins. Reports were that some of the prostitutes lingered to ask the laymen some questions about their faith while others ran away crying because they felt their sin was too great to be forgiven.

This answered my question as to the propriety of this location for the convention. There was definitely a good reason for the convention site to be there. The attendees were given many opportunities to give a strong witness of Jesus' love and forgiveness of sins in an area where it was very much needed.

One evening Mary and I went for a stroll with several other couples from the convention, including Sal and Jen. Sal and I were not propositioned because our wives were with us, but we did witness some surprising boldness on the part of some of the prostitutes as they tried to turn a trick. One young woman brazenly walked up to two men who were walking ahead of us and raised her miniskirt to reveal everything she had. The men nodded in agreement and she grabbed their hands and led them into a door in the side of the building. We had never seen anything like this in our lives.

As our group was heading back to the hotel all wide-eyed and more educated in the ways of the world than when we left, we crossed the street in front of the hotel. We were crossing in compliance with the "walk" signal. Usually Mary and I walked at the head of the foursome, but for some reason, Sal and Jen were ahead this time. A new compact sedan pulled up to the crosswalk and stopped. I noticed that its right turn signal was blinking and I expected the driver to wait until the crosswalk was clear before attempting his turn. Evidently Sal and Jen did too as they proceeded to cross in front of the car. But the driver suddenly started to make his turn then spotted the couple ahead of him and slammed on his brakes.

It was too late.

The forward motion of the car hit Sal at his knees and pushed him into Jen and the two of them went sprawling to the pavement. I was so close to the driver that I could see his eyes through the side window. I saw panic in them as they darted from side to side as though he was looking for a way to escape.

I acted instinctively and reached for the car door handle and pulled it open. The young man's foot was coming off the brake and heading for the gas pedal. Assuming he was going to attempt a getaway, I reached into the car and slammed my right foot on the brake and with the same motion jammed the shift lever into park. I pulled the youth out of the car and demanded, "Just where do you think you are going?" Simultaneously with my action three African American men who were in their twenties bolted out of the car. I feared that I was in for a pretty good thrashing, but to my surprise, they ran away.

Now I was suspicious. Something wasn't right!

Bystanders were helping Sal and Jen to their feet. Sal limped over to the curb in obvious pain. A crowd was beginning to gather and fortunately a patrolman was soon on the scene. I dragged the young driver over to the curb by his shirt and we tried to unravel the situation. He was shaking from fear.

The officer was grilling the young driver who was answering each question with, "Yes sir!" or "No sir!" His story was that, at the encouragement of his three passengers, he had "borrowed" his older brother's new car without asking him. "Does my brother have to know this happened?" he asked the policeman with trembling voice. It was obvious that he was an inexperienced driver. "I thought everything was clear so I started to make a right turn. Then I saw the couple walking in front of the car and I slammed on my brakes. Hey, they walked in front of me!"

Then pointing at me he said, "Then this guy opens my door and yanks me out of the car!"

The young driver saw an opportunity to turn some blame away from him and in my direction. He observed that Jen was all right and Sal was trying to walk off the injury to his leg. His answers were beginning to get belligerent.

I recognized that the three men who were riding with him in the car had doubled back and were mingling with the growing crowd of curiosity seekers.

The driver saw them too.

The crowd, much of which was African American, began to sympathize with the young driver and he could sense the sentiment shifting in his favor. With his pals making noises of race and prejudice, he became more and more vocal.

The officer called for backup on his radio.

Just when it seemed that things might get nasty, a handful of laymen went by. As God's providence would guide the situation, our South Dakota Regional Governor of the L.L.L. was in the group. He stood about six foot five and was an imposing figure with a full head of white hair. He recognized me and noticed that I was at the center of what was going on, so he stopped by to see if he could offer any assistance. As I explained to him the situation, I could hear the siren of the approaching police back up.

I didn't want the governor to take his precious time and get involved. With the police approaching, I thought that the situation would be resolved without further incident. So I told him, "Thanks Governor, but I think everything's in hand here. We can handle it."

He responded, "All right, Pastor Tim, but if you need any help just call on me any time."

"Thanks Governor, I will."

The eyes of the young driver got as big as headlights and he exclaimed, "You know da Governor!'

Well, it was obvious that he didn't know the governor. So I played along with his ignorance and said, "You bet I do. He is a close friend of mine." It wasn't a lie. I knew the governor.

After that, we had no more trouble from the young man or anyone in the crowd. The backup officers arrived, information was given to the policemen and the driver was taken to the station for more questioning.

A 1960's model paddy wagon arrived to take Sal and Jen to an emergency hospital to be checked over. Mary and I rode along. The paddy wagon had no windows where we sat so we had no concept of where it was taking us. The ride lasted about 15 minutes with plenty of stopping, starting and turning over bumpy streets. When we finally arrived at our destination, I observed that we were in a very dark part of town near San Francisco Bay. Blotting out the night sky was a maze of highways intersecting in a system of overpasses. We were ushered into a large three-story brick building that looked nothing like a hospital. It had a very small single door and was not, as one would expect, a big double door that would admit a gurney. There was no sign above the door identifying it as a hospital. The feeling was creepy!

The door opened into a small portico. An attendant in a white lab coat greeted us. He seemed to be the only sign of something official. He identified Sal and Jen as the injured parties and requested that Mary and I remain in the portico where there was a bench for two.

Sal and Jen disappeared down a long hallway with the man in the white coat.

I knew that things take a long time in an emergency hospital but, after what seemed like an inordinate length of time, Mary and I both became uneasy. Our conversation had waned and we became more aware of our surroundings. Both of us spotted the inlay in the tile floor of the portico at the same time. A chill ran up our backs.

It was a Nazi swastika!

I know that World War II was long over, but I was aware that there lingered an organization named Skin Heads who identified with the Nazi ideals. Now the time passed even more slowly and we became concerned for Sal and Jen. *Where were they? Were they in good hands?* The longer we waited the more my imagination went wild. *Should we storm the place? What could the two of us do? Should we call the police? Hey, they're the ones who brought us here! Can we trust them? What should we do?*

It was a good thing that we considered our options for as long as we did, because Sal and Jen finely came walking down the hallway toward us looking pretty good except for Sal's slight limp. They reported that they received good care and they had only minor cuts and bruises. The doctor told them that they would be sore for a while, but they were all right. What a relief!

I pointed to the swastika in the floor and Sal, who was well read about W.W.II passed it off saying, " There were a number of Nazi cells in the U.S.A. during the war especially in port cities. They were closely watched by the Central Intelligence Agency."

I wondered why it was never removed? Maybe the emergency hospital was a historical site. Whatever! It came close to being a "hysterical site" for us!

The same patty wagon mysteriously returned, delivered the four of us to our convention hotel and we continued the convention without further excitement.

In retrospect, we should have been more trusting in our Lord's protection in this unfamiliar territory Nazi swastika and all. After all, He did send us the "Governor" at just the right time.

Chapter 18 – Perceptions

"Stop judging by mere appearances and make a right judgment!" St. John 7:24

American author, Henry David Thoreau wrote, "Truth is in the eye of the beholder. It is a matter of perception." I agree with that statement. If a man perceives a situation a certain way and is convinced that it is truth, it is practically impossible to convince him to change his mind. If you try to change his perception, he will think that you are the liar and are trying to manipulate the truth for your own purpose.

The following year the L.L.L. Convention was held in St. Louis, Missouri. Our attendance there brought back many fond memories of our vicarage year and Mary teaching at St. Matthew Lutheran Church during parts of 1963 and 1964.

Mary and I had our mobile home moved to St. Louis for a year of vicarage. I was to serve as a student and assistant to Pastor Edward Franz at St. Matthew Lutheran Church and Mary was to teach second grade in their school.

We both had many good times there and grew very much in our learning and faith. I recall a situation when I was called upon to make a hospital visit. One of our members, named Fred, had been in pain for a few days without knowing the cause. Then his appendix burst, giving him relief for a while until peritonitis began to set in. He was rushed to the hospital and into emergency surgery. It must have been his wife who called the church wanting someone to visit and pray with him.

By the time I arrived at the hospital Fred was out of surgery and in recovery. I entered the recovery area and went to his bedside, which was nestled in a small cubicle. He was still under the anesthetic when I arrived, but I knew that people who appear unconscious may still able to hear. So I prayed out loud.

As I prayed, his eyes opened a little. They grew big with a startled look as he saw me and then gradually returned to normal. He slipped back under the effects of the anesthetic and went to sleep. A nurse slipped into the room to check his vital signs and she assured me that he was going to recover but he just needed to rest. I had accomplished the requested prayer so I left my clergy card as a reminder that I had been there and returned to the church.

About a week later, I stopped by to visit Fred at his home to see how he was recovering. He was doing very well but I was surprised to see that he was wearing one of his wife's dresses. I didn't mention it as I thought the explanation would come sooner or later. I thought he looked kind of cute in it if a man can look cute in a dress. It was a pink print of some kind and it brought out the color in his cheeks.

Fred greeted me warmly and invited me to sit down. He looked at me for a few seconds and started to laugh. He explained, "Vicar, when you came to visit me in the hospital I was just coming out of the anesthetic and my first conscious remembrance was of a voice praying above me. My first thought was that I had died and gone to heaven and that you were an angel. Then I woke up enough to open my eyes and what I saw startled me. There was a figure standing over my bed with hands folded in prayer. A round light shown from behind him that perfectly encircled his head. It looked like an angel with a halo. When my eyes finally adjusted to the light, I was so relieved to see it was you and I wasn't dead that I must have relaxed. The anesthetic took over and I fell back to sleep."

I responded, "Fred, that is a very clear recollection of events while being under the influence of an anesthetic."

"Well, at first when I woke up, I thought it was a dream. Then a nurse told me that you had been here to visit, I found your card and I gradually pieced things together. It took me a while though."

"I'm glad you figured it out and I'm flattered to think that you thought I was an angel. That's the first time anyone has considered me angelic!"

"You were an angel to me that day in the hospital and I want to thank you for being there."

"I'm glad that you believed you were in heaven and not in hell."

"Me too! By the words of your prayer I knew I was in heaven and not that other place."

As we continued our visit, Fred finally unraveled the reason for the dress. "I suppose you're wondering why I have my wife's dress on."

The thought had occurred to me.

"As a result of my surgery I have to wear a colostomy bag strapped to my waist. Because of the bag, I can't wear pants with a belt, so I borrowed one of Meta's housedresses. Yesterday I was getting cabin fever and decided to go outside and do some weeding. As people drove by on heavily traveled Florissant Avenue they did a double take at a man with hairy legs bending over wearing a dress. I nearly caused six accidents. It never entered my mind that I might be such a distraction. Now I keep my weeding to the back yard."

"That's a good thing," I said. We both had a good laugh.

When I returned to the church, I told Pastor Franz about Fred's excitement. He responded by telling me a story about a former custodian of the church. I didn't get the connection between Fred and the custodian except that it was close to the Easter season.

He told me it happened two years ago on Easter Sunday morning. It was the custodian's responsibility to ring the church bells thirty minutes before the first worship service and again at the hour church was to begin. Members claimed they heard the first tolling of the bells, but they were strangely silent when the service began. Pastor Franz explained to me that in order to ring the bells, one had to go through a narrow door and then climb a stepladder fixed to the wall. The bell rope was located in a small room, which housed the organ pipes directly above the location of the choir. A screen separated the room from the congregation but allowed sounds to flow into the church freely. I had an idea of where the story was heading.

Unknown to anyone, the custodian had "celebrated" a little too much on Saturday night. His alarm clock woke him on Sunday morning and realizing his responsibility to ring the bells, he got out of bed and groggily trudged off to church to perform his duty. After ringing the bell the first time he passed out in the little room and lay there through the first part of the service. The timing was just right that when Pastor Franz was preaching about Jesus rising from the dead, moans were heard echoing through the church.

"Oooooooh! Ooooooooooh! Oooooooooooooooooh!"

With startled looks, people searched to see where the moans were coming from. Some members said they interpreted them to be sound effects planned by Pastor Franz to add emphasis to Jesus rising from the dead.

The trustees weren't so convinced. Several of them exited the service at the back of the church and began the search for the source of the groaning. They had their suspicions and quickly converged at the small door, which was ajar. Upon climbing the ladder, they found the inebriated custodian passed out on the floor still uttering groans.

Needless to say, that custodian did not have to worry about getting up in the morning to ring the church bell ever again. He had been warned repeatedly concerning his drinking problem. There would be no more chances. Any perception of his job security at St. Matthew ended with this incident.

Another false perception took place in Columbia, South Dakota while I was serving three churches.

On Sundays I conducted three services, all in the morning. Since there wasn't much time between services and a 20-minute drive separated each church, I left my preaching robes on as I traveled. I finished the second service in Groton and made the trip back to Columbia with a few minutes to spare. As I drove through the main street of town, I noticed a member's car parked outside the local tavern. I had noticed the car there on previous Sunday mornings and thought the owner should be in church, but I didn't have the extra time to stop and deal with it.

This Sunday morning, I did.

I parked on the street in front of the establishment, never once considering what the church members might think if they saw me entering that bar. I had only one thing on my mind, to chastise that member for being there on Sunday morning and encourage him to get to church. Fully vested in cassock, surplice and stole, I entered the building. The offending member was standing behind the bar drying some glasses. When he saw me he nearly dropped one and his mouth opened, but nothing came out.

I shook my finger at him and chastised, "This is not where you should be on Sunday morning. With your terminal cancer you need to be in church making sure that you have a strong relationship with your Lord!" Not giving him a chance to respond, I turned around and headed back to my car and drove on to St. John's.

The worship service progressed. My perspective from a pulpit that was raised about 6 steps above the level of the congregation revealed the expressions on the faces of the members. Part way into the message I observed Harvey, who was sitting about half way back on the pulpit side of the church, with his arms folded over his chest. The look of contempt on his face couldn't have been clearer. I realized that something was amiss.

After the service I greeted the members at the door and it wasn't long before Harvey stood next in line. It was obvious that I was going to find out what was bugging him right then and there, as he still had this tight-jaw look on his face. I reached out to shake his hand but he refused. "What's the matter, Preacher? Do you have to stop and have a belt before you come and preach to us?" Harvey demanded.

It suddenly became clear. He saw me coming out of the tavern and perceived that I had a drink. I replied with a knowing smile on my face, " You may not believe this, but I would never consider having a drink on Sunday morning. I saw a member's car parked in front of the tavern and I went in to make a mission call to urge him to come to church!" Harvey's countenance fell as, I'm sure, he too recognized the same member's car in front of the bar and a similar thought had run through his mind. Without another word, he hung his head as he realized the frivolity of his perception and disappeared in disgrace.

I have often wondered how many other members saw me coming out of that bar and never considered asking me about it.

These examples are reminders that we must never jump to conclusions. For the things that we see with our eyes and hear with our ears may not be what they seem. Therefore, it is important to get all of the facts and listen to all the input we can get before we make any assumptions. Our patience in such matters can save us from embarrassment and disclose our wisdom.

Pastor Tim and Mary in front of St. Matthew Lutheran Church at St. Louis, Missouri while on vicarage.

Chapter 19 – A Donkey's Last Laugh

"Do not be like the horse or like the donkey, which have no understanding, which must be harnessed with bit and bridle." Psalm 32:8-11

I have often said, "Whatever works!" meaning some situations may have several possible solutions and someone must choose the one that will work. Generally speaking, that's not always an easy position to be in. But when you are the shepherd of the flock, people will look to you for the correct solution. Sometimes you can buy a little time until there is more information by saying, "Whatever works!" It sounds like a decision has been made; but actually, it offers more time for review. If it saves someone from making an embarrassing decision, so be it.

The following situation is a good example of "Whatever works." The youth of Peace Lutheran Church in Rapid City put on a Christmas pageant every December that depicted the birth of Jesus. It was called a Living Nativity, complete with scriptural narration and Christmas carols. A stable scene was set up in the church parking lot, hay was brought in for the live sheep that would be with the shepherds on the "hillside near Bethlehem," and a donkey was used to carry Mary from Nazareth to Bethlehem.

In previous years the youth borrowed a docile donkey from Wildcat Cave that was accustomed to people. But this year, when the authorities at the cave were contacted, they said the donkey was unavailable because it was too old and sick.

Panic!

The young lady, who was to play Mary, knew someone from whom she could borrow a replacement donkey. She made the request and she had her transportation to Bethlehem.

Everything was ready for the first night's performance. When the owners of the donkey dropped him off, everyone was amazed at the sight of that beautiful animal. Compared to the short little dark-brown donkey from the cave, this one stood five-feet tall and was all white. He was a beautiful specimen but that soon caused a problem.

The production was moving along very well until it was time for Mary to climb on the donkey's back and ride to Bethlehem. We had anticipated the problem of her getting onto the donkey's back and had devised a system of two steps borrowed from the church's drinking fountain. Our good plan broke down when Mary climbed the steps and tried to mount the donkey. He took a step sideways and Mary slid off. Joseph looked over his shoulder, shrugged and trotted off leading the donkey with Mary walking behind. The same scene happened at performances two and three.

It was time for the Christmas Eve performance and the donkey's owners were going to be in the audience. Mary was determined to show the owners that she could ride on the donkey's back. We came up with a plan that Joseph would lean with all of his weight against the donkey so that he couldn't move away from the mounting Mary. She would run up the steps and jump on the donkey's back. As I said, she was a determined young lady and I had every confidence that she could do it. But, just in case she came flying over the donkey's back, a strong stagehand was ready to run out of the shadows to try and catch her before she hit the ground.

As usual, the pageant was moving along without incident. The time arrived for Mary to mount the donkey. Everyone was in place. The youth were tense. Joseph braced himself against the donkey. Mary ran up the steps and took a flying leap. But the donkey was too strong for Joseph; he was still able to move away from Mary who was flying through the air. She landed with a thud on the donkey's back, her head and arms on one side and her legs on the other. Joseph looked over his shoulder, shook his head and led Mary "dead man" style on to Bethlehem.

It wasn't funny at the time, but as we looked back on the picture in our minds we realized how funny it looked. The owners of the donkey thought it was hilarious.

Later, that donkey redeemed himself.

A church member, named Geoffrey, who lived in the country, was to return the donkey to its owners following the last performance. By the time he got the donkey loaded into his truck, it was already eleven o'clock and he thought it was too late to return the donkey that night. So, he drove home and tied him to the bumper of a truck, which was parked near a mobile home that his mother lived in.

During the night a fire broke out in the mobile home. The donkey made so much noise with his "Hee Hawing" and attempts at trying to pull away from the fire that it woke Geoffrey. He was able to wake up his mother and get her out of the burning mobile home uninjured.

The donkey was now a hero.

Geoffrey told me the story when he came to church for the Christmas Day service. The account fit well into my sermon as an illustration of how God can provide miracles through unlikely means. Who would ever guess that an uncooperative donkey would save a person's life on Christmas Eve?

When God sent His only son into the world, born of humble parents in a lowly stable, many overlooked Him as the Savior of all. But God's plan was so simple that everyone without regard to financial position or ethnic background could receive Him. In effect, God said, "Whatever works!" And His plan has worked for centuries and will continue to work until He comes on the last day to take all believers to heaven.

Chapter 20 – The Formation of Peace

"I hear that when you come together as a church, there are divisions among you...No doubt there have to be divisions among you to show which of you have God's approval." I Corinthians 11:18-19

It is not always easy to bring two congregations together to become one, however, Peace Lutheran Church of Rapid City made the transition. It was not without some frustrations and adjustments among the members. But to Peace's credit, I have heard of church members else where in congregations who got out their shotguns to ward off any pastors who might have similar plans for their church.

For many years Ascension and St. Luke's Lutheran Churches existed in two separate locations of Rapid City. St. Luke's had been formed first and served as a friendly neighborhood congregation in a southern section of the city called Robinsdale. Ascension was a newer mission congregation nestled on a hill in the north part of town. It had been initially designed to be a mission to the Ogalala Sioux Indians that primarily lived in that part of town. The Indians, however, weren't attracted to the formal style of Lutheran worship in any great numbers, so the congregation grew into a close-knit group of worshipers living in the north part of town.

Since neither congregation was very large, usually the same pastor served both. In 1969, the congregations began to discuss the possibility of joining together into one church. Numerous meetings were held that went long into the night. Many issues had to be decided like, which facility would they use and how the organizations would be joined. The agreement was finally reached to use St. Luke's building and that all organizations would join together except for the two ladies groups. The reason was that each group had their own special purpose. The St. Luke's ladies strongly supported The Lutheran Woman's Missionary League mission of reaching out to the world with the Gospel of Christ. The Ascension ladies, while also subscribing to The LWML, had as their purpose serving and aiding their congregation to minister to the members and community. It was felt that the purposes of these two organizations both had great merit and could peacefully coexist.

The name agreed upon for the new congregation was to be Peace Lutheran Church, in order to represent the unity expressed by the joining of the two congregations.

The pastor before me did an excellent job of helping the two diverse congregations hammer out the details of the consolidation. But he realized that his ministry there represented much angst, and that for the congregation to thrive and grow, he needed to step out of the way. Honorably he accepted a call to his home state of Minnesota. Some months later I accepted the call to the new Peace Lutheran Church. Everything seemed poised to grow and, on the surface, all seemed calm.

During the weeks following my installation, the elders came to me and announced that there was a problem festering between the two ladies organizations. Their differing philosophies were causing problems. I called a joint meeting of the LWML and Ladies Aid for Sunday after the church service. As we gathered in the meeting room, the feelings on the surface seemed cordial. I asked each organization to outline their purpose and goals and then asked for discussion on where the differences lay. The purposes of each organization flowed freely but, when we got to the crux of the problem, everyone clamed up. I encouraged several of the ladies whom I had come to realize were the leaders of their respective groups to share their feelings. The LWML leaders shared their belief that the Ladies Aid should take more of an interest in the worldwide mission of the church. While the Ladies Aid felt that the LWML group should take more interest in aiding the ministry of Peace Lutheran.

When they were finished expressing their views, I summarized what they had said and explained that there was room for both purposes at Peace. Our church had a need for ladies to focus on the local ministry as well as the church-at-large needed ladies to adopt the worldwide mission of the church. I further counseled them that I saw no reason the two ladies organizations could not peacefully coexist with different goals. In fact, that was a good arrangement because two ladies organizations working toward the same purpose could certainly lock horns. In a respectful tone I laid down the rule, "As long as I am pastor here, I want you both to support each other's purpose and to get along. I don't want to hear any bickering or undercutting of each other's ministries." To this they agreed. But to make sure all went well my wife joined both organizations. I also served as pastoral advisor to both groups demonstrating that I supported their respective ministries. For the most part peace reigned between the ladies groups during my six-year ministry there.

My mistake was in telling them, "that while I was their pastor, they must work together." Because, after I took a call, my successor reported that the same problem raised its ugly head and had to be dealt with all over again. I understand that peace now reigns at Peace.

The following situation that united the two congregations into one was a gift from God. Peace congregation began to experience a large influx of new members. This often happens in a growing neighborhood where people visit the church or watch from a distance, but wait to change their membership until they find out what type of pastor the newly called shepherd will be. Two months into my ministry there, I planned a worship service to include the reception of new members. Members were noticing that the church was growing more full on Sunday morning, but none of them were prepared for the numbers of new members that came forward to the altar that day. About a third of the worshippers got up and came forward to be received as new members. There was an audible gasp from the remaining members who were seated in the pews and I could almost read their thoughts. *We'd better get our act together and befriend all these new members and incorporate them into our church before they take over!* And that's exactly what they did.

From that day, Peace Lutheran congregation became unified in its purpose and the members reached out in friendliness to the community welcoming everyone who came through its doors. It was known in the district as the friendly church and it continued to grow. It was the fastest growing Lutheran Church-Missouri Synod congregation in the state of South Dakota from 1971 through 1977. In 1975 an addition was built on to the church that doubled its seating capacity, added four classrooms and a large parish hall with a modern kitchen. But the church's friendly members were the church's biggest assets.

Chapter 21 – Peace Family Campout

"A shout for help brought their partners in the other boat and soon both boats were filled with fish and on the verge of sinking." St. Luke 5:7

One activity that demonstrates the unity that came to Peace Lutheran was its annual Family Campout at Sheridan Lake in the beautiful Black Hills. A large portion of the congregation participated in the campouts from their inception.

Our family participated in the first campout held the last weekend in June. We considered tenting but that didn't excite us very much. We all preferred to be up off the cold, hard ground. So, we searched the classified adds in the newspaper. We settled on a neat little pop-up tent camper that we bought second hand. It had a double bed at each end of the camper covered with a three-inch foam mattress, but it was still more comfortable than being on the ground. Fortunately our children were small enough that all three could sleep in sleeping bags on the same bed.

Drilling a hole in the frame of our car for the trailer hitch was no easy task using a borrowed drill and a dull bit, but I got the job done. Compared to the drilling, the wiring for the taillights was a breeze. We were very proud of our first camping rig.

We drove up to the Sheridan Lake campsite and were all settled in a nice shady spot by mid-afternoon. Then we sat back and enjoyed watching the other campers gradually filtering in with everything from sleeping bags to luxury motor homes. Everyone had arrived before darkness set in, except for one family with three children. We wondered if they had changed their minds or if something serious came up that prevented their coming. As it turned out the head of the family had to work later than expected, and then they had to rent a tent.

It was dark by the time the headlights of the Mc Nutley's station wagon appeared over the hill and came to rest in the middle of the campsite. It seemed like pandemonium broke loose in the serenity of our campsite when the Mc Nutley family burst out of their vehicle all at the same time and scurried around looking for a place to pitch their tent. Each one of them had a different idea of where it should go. It seemed like an eternity before a consensus was reached and the tent was unloaded from the station wagon. Mr. Mc Nutley and the older boys unfolded it on the ground, and then searched for 15 minutes for their flashlight. Then by the faint beam of the flashlight, they studied the directions on how to set up the tent. Some of the campers who had experience in setting up tents offered to help, but Mr. Mc Nutley turned down the offer politely saying that it would be a good learning experience for the children.

The volunteers settled back around the campfire to observe the tent set up. However, it turned out to be much more than just observation—it was entertainment!

Mr. Mc Nutley ordered his boys to get the tent poles out of the wagon. There was a lot of clanging and banging on the station wagon, the ground and each other; it looked like a scene from a Marx brother's movie. In the beam of the flashlight Mc Nutley was still trying to figure out the directions for the configuration of the tent poles. When he thought that he had it all figured out, he began barking out directions to the family. "I think I've figured it out! Bring this pole here. That one goes there. This one fits in here. That's it. Now fit this one into here and that should be it."

It looked sturdy enough, but as soon as Mc Nutley let go, the frame crashed to the ground. "Let's start over," he commanded as he studied the directions some more. This time the frame held and the order was given to throw the canvass tent over the frame. Everything was progressing well until the entire Mc Nutley family clamored into the tent to try and secure it to the poles and it came crashing down on all of them. There was a disappointed groan from inside the fallen tent, a few harsh words of blame and a lot of scurrying taking place. Finally Mc Nutley heads popped out of the tent door one by one. Each one's hair was messed up and they looked like they had slept in it. Their faces showed frustration as the flames from the campfire reflected on their rosy cheeks. There was a flash of determination in their eyes that communicated they were not about to give up until they had mastered that tent. Especially with everyone watching them.

The spectators watched with amusement, struggling with little success to stifle their laughs. This made the family even more determined in their quest to raise that tent. With renewed effort they struggled together having learned from their past failure.

At last, it appeared like the tent frame would hold. The canvas was stretched over the frame and it held. Finally, as the tent stakes were being driven into the ground with great determination, it seemed like the Mc Nutley's problems were over.

Not quite.

Mrs. Mc Nutley ordered the two boys to get the blankets out of the station wagon. After a long absence they returned with long faces and reported, "The blankets aren't in the car. Where are they?"

"John, didn't you put them in the car like I told you?" Mrs. Mc Nutley questioned the oldest son.

"I asked Jen to do it!"

"Oh no!" cried the mother, "They must still be at home. What'll we do now?"

It wasn't long before the Mc Nutley family was soliciting each camper asking, "Can you spare just one blanket for tonight?"

Who could resist helping this forlorn family that had provided so much entertainment.

Early the next morning, as the sun began to peek through the trees, it was the Mc Nutley family that was up first. They were trying to start a fire to get warm and make some coffee. Starting the fire was another circus for them as the wood was wet from the overnight rain.

Finally they got the fire started and the coffee was hot by the time the rest of us were ready to climb out of our warm beds. Soon the smell of bacon and eggs wafted through the campsite and hungry campers ravaged the prepared food. The day was spent in a variety of activities consisting of swimming, canoeing, hiking or visiting around the campfire.

That evening as the campfire crackled, the children made S'mores while adults played cards. Everyone was relaxed and having a wonderful time and no one noticed some voices in the distance. They were imperceptible at first, and then gradually became clearer. Others who weren't occupied with activities began to wonder if it was some kind of call for help. "Shush!" someone said, "Listen to those voices crying down by the lake!"

As the noise in the camp quieted to a hush, the voices became louder. First there was the baritone voice of a man crying out, **"Help!"** Following the man's voice was that of a youth noticeably higher in pitch, "Help!" The yells came in rapid succession and alternated from baritone to high tenor.

"Help!" Help!" **"Help!"** "Help!" **"Help!"** "Help!"

At first it sounded like a fake distress call, but the longer we listened, the more frantic the voices became.

Some of our campers started running toward the lake. Because of the darkness, I drove my car down to the lake in order to shine the headlights out over the water to see what was happening. As the headlights played out over the water, they revealed a partially submerged boat and nine people thrashing about in the water about 50 yards off shore. The marina operators heard the cries in their cabin nearby and had returned to the dock. They started their motorboat to go out and retrieve the floundering family. It took them three trips, but all were brought to shore safely.

Peace members brought towels and blankets and poured hot coffee into them as the family related what had happened and how foolish they had been.

They had been in their boat for a good part of the evening. It had a capacity of six persons and they had squeezed in nine. They didn't want to leave any of their party behind, so they risked it. As they rode around the lake, each time they slowed down, water flowed over the covered transom into the boat. No one realized what was happening. As they approached the shore and throttled down one more time, the boat took on enough water that it began to sink, dropping everyone into the lake as darkness set in.

The family realized how foolish they were in not taking the precaution to wear the life jackets. When the boat began to sink, the life jackets that were stowed under the deck were out of reach. Some of the younger children couldn't swim and began to sink. As if guided by the Lord's hand, the adults reached into the blackness of the water and pulled two of them to the surface by their hair. They all clung to the overturned boat.

The owner of the boat began to yell; "**Help!**" and his ten-year-old son joined him, "Help!" They could see the lights of the campfires on shore and wondered why no one was coming to their rescue. After a while they realized how their cries for help must have sounded to those on shore and only the man shouted.

By the time the marina boat reached them, they had been in the water yelling for almost an hour. By God's grace, every family member was found clinging to the boat.

The family was very appreciative to the members of Peace Lutheran Church for our care and compassion in their time of need. To show their appreciation, they all attended worship at our church the next Sunday, distributed gifts and expressed their gratitude to our wonderful people.

We were thankful that the Lord put us there to help them and everyone was spared, but we wished we had taken seriously their calls for help and responded more promptly.

Chapter 22 – The Undercover Groom

"... Each of us will give an account of himself to God. Therefore let us stop passing judgment on one another." Romans 14:12-13

For a reason that I never could understand, the weddings that I performed at Peace Lutheran Church often had a strange twist to them. I learned that the answers to some of my questions in the premarital counseling could have unique repercussions.

It was the first session with Alice and Bill who had decided to get married in July. Alice was our member and I knew her and her family very well. The groom, however, was not familiar to me at all. So, to get acquainted, I casually asked him some questions.

"Do you live here in Rapid City?"

"Yes," Bill replied, "I have lived here for about four years."

"Where was your home before that?"

"I came here from Indiana where my parents live."

"What do you do for a living, Bill?"

What happened next put me a little on the edge of my chair. Bill didn't answer right away, but looked to the door of my office obviously checking to see if anyone was out there listening. Then he asked, "May I close the door?"

It was obvious that I was going to hear something confidential so I answered, "Of course."

After the door was closed, Bill asked me, " Can you keep this absolutely confidential?"

"Certainly!" I answered and I wondered what was coming next. *Was he an escaped convict? Was Bill a bank robber or was he a hit man?* My thoughts ran all over the gamut of what might be. So, I was relieved when he lifted the shroud of doubt by saying, "I'm an undercover agent for the Alcohol, Tobacco and Firearms Unit of the Rapid City Police Department."

All I could say in response was, "Oh!"

"Now you can understand why it is so essential that this is kept confidential."

"How did you get into that line of work?"

"I used drugs. I did crack. I got busted a few years back and received treatment and came out clean. Because I know how the drug-user's mind works and I understand their language, the ATF asked if I would be willing to go to work for them. I agreed."

"That's pretty dangerous work. It is obvious that Alice knows what you do. Are you accepting of Bill's line of work, Alice?"

Alice nodded her head, but looked a little nervous about it.

Bill went on, "I'm about to finger a large drug ring here in Rapid City. By the time it hits the newspapers, Alice and I will be on our honeymoon and then we'll move on to another town to clean up the drugs there. But I'm glad you asked me what I do, Pastor, because it was necessary for me to invite some drug dealers to the wedding so that I don't blow my cover. I thought you should be aware of that."

All right! Now how do I handle this? I can see it now in The Rapid City Journal; "Police raid Lutheran Church while a wedding was in progress. Police received a tip that known local drug traffickers and users were gathered for a wedding at Peace Lutheran Church. Police also arrested the pastor as an accessory."

The day of the wedding arrived. Everyone was scurrying around with the last minute preparations. The bride and her bridesmaids were dressed, the groom and his groomsmen had arrived, and the guests were beginning to file into the church. I went to make a final check of the church to make sure everything was in its place and I noticed something that made my heart beat faster. One of the ushers, who I thought was a little strange at the rehearsal, was acting loud and boisterous as he ushered the guests down the side aisle. He certainly was not following the instruction given to the ushers the night before.

Suddenly it hit me. The usher was a drug user and he was high as a kite!

I looked around the wedding party for the biggest and strongest man I could find. He was also an usher and the brother-in-law of the bride. I went over to him and pointed to the "high" usher and told him in a hushed tone, "If he steps out of line at all, I want you to grab him and escort him out the door and don't let him back into the church."

As I continued with the business of the wedding preparations, thoughts of that usher faded from my mind. I totally lost track of him so, evidently, he was behaving. It wasn't until I finished the wedding sermon that he drew my attention again.

I spotted him sitting directly behind the bride's parents as he began loudly applauding my sermon. People starred at him and, with an embarrassed grin, he slowly dropped his hands.

After the wedding I lost track of him again. He disappeared and left the responsibility of escorting the families and guests from the church to the other two ushers.

The "notorious" usher reappeared at the reception. He was sitting at the end of one of the tables with a stack of money in front of him asking people, "Do you want to make a buy?"

Fortunately no one was paying much attention to him.

I was in a sticky situation. If I called the police, I risked blowing the groom's cover and putting the pending drug bust in jeopardy. If I did nothing and someone else called the police, I risked my imaginary headlines coming true.

I prayed, *Gracious Lord, keep the eyes closed of those who do not understand what is happening here. Keep them ignorant of the type of transaction this drug dealer is trying to make. Help them to ignore him. And Lord, help this wedding reception to get over soon!*

The Lord heard my prayer and the reception was the shortest in my experience. And if anyone ever figured out what the drug-dealing usher was doing, no one ever said a word to me.

Two days after the wedding the Rapid City Journal carried a full account of a major drug bust that took place in town. The article related that an undercover agent had infiltrated the drug organization exposing the names of the leaders. It was the largest drug ring exposed in Rapid City up to that time and it cleaned up the city's drug trafficking for some time. I was relieved that my name did not appear in the article.

I never saw the undercover groom and his bride again.

Chapter 23 – You Never Know About Prospect Visits

The wisdom of the prudent is to give thought to their ways, but the folly of fools is deception." Proverbs 14:8

I never wanted a mundane job where every day was the same. My dream was fulfilled when I became a pastor. Each day of my ministry was filled with its own unique surprises always new and different. My challenge was to meet each new day with adaptability, a sense of humor and guidance from my Lord.

On a sunny summer Sunday morning I welcomed a good-looking young couple that visited our church for the first time. I was especially struck by the good looks of the woman, who I guessed, was in her early thirties. She had flowing blonde wavy hair and blue eyes that matched the powder blue tailored suit she was wearing. I'm always excited when a young couple enters the door of our church because they represent the future of the church and have the potential to become leaders and to build the Sunday school by having children.

Perhaps I was over eager to make a visit on this couple.

As soon as I could break away from business at the church on Monday, I was knocking at the door of the address the couple had written in the guest book. I am usually pretty good at recognizing faces, but when the doorbell was answered, I was staring into the face of someone I did not recognize at all! My first thoughts were d*o I have the right house? Maybe there's another lady living here?*

The lady had short dishwater-blonde hair and her eyes were gray and not the pretty blue I had observed on Sunday. However, experience had taught me that colored contact lenses are able to change eye color drastically. Her face was rounder than I remembered and she had a somewhat ruddy complexion that I knew could be remedied by makeup. She was wearing a sweatshirt that didn't allow for any judgment of approximate weight.

I felt guilty for even wondering.

The only similarity with the lady in church on Sunday was her height, and I could have misjudged that. After all, one can only observe and digest so much of a person on a brief first meeting. And I thought that I had done amazingly well, perhaps too well.

To my surprise, this lady recognized me right away. She said, "I'm so glad that you dropped by, Pastor, and I am especially pleased that you came on Monday so soon after we visited. That impresses me and tells me that you're eager to have new members join your church." She invited me in and motioned me to sit on the couch.

I was still trying to get my bearings so that I might identify this woman. She evidently knew me and must have been in church recently, but I didn't recognize her at all. I fished around as we visited, but nothing was being resolved in my mind. As I looked around the house for some clue to the identity of this woman, my gaze fell upon a ten by twelve portrait that I recognized immediately as the attractive woman that had been in church with her husband the day before. I was cautious, however, not wanting to make a big mistake as I sat on the couch and patiently tried to make a comparison between the lady before me and the lady in the portrait.

There was no comparison, I was sure of it.

Finally I was bold enough to ask. "Who's the young lady in the picture over there?" I was guessing it was her younger sister and I was praying that I was disguising the excitement in my voice at recognizing the person in the picture.

She flushed with embarrassment and confessed, "That's my high school graduation picture. Since then I have put on a few pounds and my hair color has darkened. On Sunday I wore a wig and when I dress up and put on makeup I can come close to resembling that picture. I'm sorry Pastor. I thought you looked somewhat confused when I answered the door, but I thought you recognized me."

My "poker face" had gotten me by this far but now I fumbled around in my mind for some words to get out of this situation safely. Finally I replied, " You did look very much like your high school picture on Sunday. Not every woman can look 10 years younger with such little effort."

She looked pleased and must have bought it, because the couple joined the church.

On another occasion I was making an evening prospect visit to a family that appeared to be doing well financially by the appearance of their home. I was seated very comfortably on the sofa facing a family of four. Before me sat a neatly groomed husband, wife and two children, a boy and a girl. The children were neat, polished like they were going to a birthday party and were using their best manners. It was obvious they were trying to impress the visiting pastor and they were doing a fine job of it too. It felt a little uneasy because it is usually the pastor who must do the impressing. It was a nice turn around.

As our amiable visit progressed, I noticed, ever so subtly, two Siamese cats crouched at the top of the stairs that led to the second floor. They had their eyes fixed on me and I felt a little uncomfortable. However, our visit continued as the parents asked some questions about the church. As I tried my best to answer them, the cats moved half way down the steps and sat down with their stare still transfixed on me. Gradually the questions moved to the subject of what programs we had to offer their children. As I answered the cats continued their move down the stairs and were now sitting in the middle of the living room still staring at me.

I am usually good at reading animals, but these cats were not about to give me the satisfaction of figuring out their intentions. As our visit continued, the cats simultaneously made one more move to within a yard from my feet and continued their noncommittal stare.

I absolutely could not read the look in those two cats eyes. I thought it was curiosity. I slowly reached my hand toward the two cats so that they could catch my scent and understand that I wasn't afraid of them and they had no reason to fear me. As I did so, the man of the house warned me, "Don't do that! They will tear your hand to shreds in a second."

I eased back slowly into the sofa and kept an eye on the cats. They observed me for a few minutes more and, after they were satisfied that they had checked me out sufficiently, turned and ran back up the stairs and disappeared.

This family didn't join our church and I never knew if they weren't impressed with our church programs, or I didn't pass the inspection of the cats.

Sometimes you never know.

Chapter 24 – Appearance of the Naked Neighbor

"Because of this I will weep and wail; I will go about barefoot and naked...Pass on in nakedness and shame you who live in Shaphir." Micah 1:8, 11

The pastor and congregation are part of a neighborhood community with which they must coexist. Sometimes that peaceful coexistence is compromised by the congregation and at other times by the neighbors. This time it was a neighbor.

A series of events began on a summer evening while Mary and I were attending a Sunday school Teacher's meeting in the church parish hall. Our three children, who were in kindergarten, first and second grades, were with us quietly coloring on a table in an opposite corner of the room. Mary noticed them climb down from their chairs to peer out the full-length window. Something outside had attracted their attention. In an instant they appeared next to us, interrupted our meeting and with eyes as big as headlights our oldest daughter announced, "Daddy! There is a man outside that pulled down his pants and is…!" Before she could finish, some of the teachers rushed to look out of the windows and others ran out of the two doors to try and spot and apprehend the culprit. But as mysteriously as he had appeared to the children, he disappeared. I believed that it must have been someone in the neighborhood for him to vanish so quickly. My suspicions were realized when I visited with the neighbor lady who lived across the street. I had observed an unmarked car parked next to their house with a man who seemed to be observing something. I asked Mrs. Gohmer, "Have you noticed that car parked over there?"

"Don't you know what's going on in the neighborhood?" She asked in disbelief.

"No, I guess I don't. Please, fill me in."

"For some time I've watched that neighbor living there doing some strange things. Last week as the children were coming home from school I saw him through my kitchen window. When the older girls would pass by his house, he would stand in his picture window with no pants on and do a little dance to try and attract their attention. I never saw any of the girls look over at his window, which seemed to frustrate him. The next thing I knew, he ran out his back door stark naked and laid over the trunk of his car parked in the driveway. The girls, who were talking animatedly didn't notice him.

Now he appeared to be even more agitated and he got into his car and drove off without a stitch on. I have no idea where he went or where he kept his car keys."

"What happened next?"

"He must have driven around for about 10 minutes and then he came back and disappeared into his house."

"Did you do anything?"

"Of course! I called the police immediately. They sent an officer out to interview me and that's why we have the plain clothes officer doing the stake out." *Mrs. Gohmer seemed very familiar with police jargon,* I thought.

"Mrs. Gohmer, would you please keep me informed about what's happening?"

The presence of the officer in the unmarked car was pretty obvious. I doubted that the neighbor would try any more tricks with him parked in front of the house. It wasn't very long before Mrs. Gohmer waved to me as I pulled into my driveway. I walked over to her yard and she gave me her report.

"This afternoon a police car with two uniformed officers drove up and arrested our "interesting" neighbor. They led him out of his house in handcuffs and put him the back of the police car and drove away. Oh! And this time he had clothes on."

Several weeks later I read in The Rapid City Journal that he had been found guilty of lewd and indecent conduct and was sentenced to six months in jail along with intensive psychiatric counseling.

It must have been about nine months later that Mary and I were shopping at J C Penney's moonlight madness sale around nine in the evening. I was deeply engrossed in digging through a pile of dress shirts on sale, when a voice next to me said, "Hi there!" I looked up and was astonished to be standing face-to-face with the "naked neighbor". My first reaction was to look for a place to hide but, with him standing right next to me, there was no place to go. There was nothing to do but to acknowledge him.

Not wishing to embarrass him with talk about where he had been I asked, "How have you been?"

"Oh pretty good! Don't you just love these clothing sales?'

"Yes, I don't ever like to pay full price for clothes, so I shop the sales whenever I can."

"Me too! I just have a weakness for clothes. By the way, I'm moving out of the community as soon as I can. I have a job offer in Deadwood managing a restaurant. Well, happy shopping!"

As he walked toward the door, I thought, *your weakness is clothes? Oh, if you could only keep them on!*

The next day I noticed his house was up for sale, and I never saw him again. I remember thinking, *I pray that you have received the help in counseling that you needed to carry on a normal life and you are able to succeed at the fresh start of your life in Deadwood.*

It is wonderful when the Lord steps in and works everything out for His people and His church. Our children were frightened for a while and needed to have the shades pulled in their bedrooms, but they grew up unaffected by the antics of our naked neighbor. Thanks to our good and gracious Lord.

Chapter 25 - Solution to a Domestic Disturbance

"Let us then approach the throne of grace with confidence, so that we may receive mercy and find grace to help in time of need." Hebrews 4: 16

When a pastor is called out during the night for a domestic disturbance one never knows what he might run into. There is always the potential that the pastor could be caught between the couple and both could turn on him. It's always wise to have some kind of back up plan.

Mary and I were getting ready for bed while watching the news on television, so it must have been past 10 P.M. The phone rang and I gave Mary a questioning look wondering what kind of situation was about to unfold at this time of night. I picked up the phone and the voice of a concerned mother from across the state met my ears.

"My name is Sandy. My son Andy and his wife Betty live in Rapid City and are members of your church."

"Yes, I know them."

"I just got off the phone with my son and something that isn't quite right. I could hear his wife yelling at him in the background. Andy seemed calm, but his tone of voice sounded strange and he was in a hurry to have me hang up. I just know that something is going on between them and he doesn't want me to know. Would you mind going over to their place to check on them?"

"Of course I'll be glad to. Would you give me a phone number where I could call you to report back?"

Sandy gave me her phone number and before she hung up said, "Oh, thank you very much for going over there. I'm so worried about them. This is the first time they've been away from family support and they speak so highly of you and your church."

"Sandy, I'll get back to you as soon as possible. If there is nothing serious going on it may not be until morning, so if you don't hear from me try not to worry," and I hung up the phone.

Mary had been listening to my side of the conversation, but I filled her in on the mother's concern. "I don't know what I'll be getting into at Andy and Betty's, so if I don't call you by 11:30, call the police department and have them send a car over to check on the situation."

Those are not particularly comforting words to say to your wife before you leave on this type of call at night, but I knew she would be in earnest prayer for me until I called her. Having the Lord as a back up is the best anyone can have, so I prayed for wisdom to deal with whatever I might find and asked the Lord to guide my words and actions. I pulled on my clothes and headed over to Andy and Betty's home.

It's always wise to consider all possibilities and try to anticipate what might happen. If they had been drinking, their problems might be attributed to that. Andy was about my size but, if he was impaired by alcohol, I figured that I could handle him physically. Now, how was I going to explain my showing up at their home at around 11 P.M.? I came up with saying, "Hello! I was just in the neighborhood and thought I would drop by to visit you." It sounded very lame, but I couldn't think of anything else.

The house was nestled on the crest of a hill on an acre of land, so it was very dark outside when I arrived. The lights were on inside the house and all seemed peaceful. I listened for a minute to see if I could hear any yelling so that I might gain some insight as to what was going on inside.

There was nothing.

When I rang the bell, Andy answered the door fairly quickly. He appeared calm and sober. In fact, he was quite cordial. I presented my lame reason for being at his door so late in the evening and he didn't buy it for a moment.

"My mother called you didn't she?"

"Yes, she was concerned about how you and Betty were getting along. She asked if I would drop by check on you both." I decided it was best to be honest.

"Come on in Pastor, my wife is upset."

As I entered, I noticed a cozy home that for the most part was neat and clean. However, a magazine rack was overturned and some books were on the floor. Betty was sitting on a recliner with her arms folded across her chest and her legs curled up under her. She was wearing a white t-shirt with blue shorts and no shoes. Her hair was messed and there was a tight expression on her face and a glint of anger in her eyes. She looked at me coolly as I came through the door and made no greeting.

Andy motioned me to sit down and he began to explain, "My wife had knee surgery a week ago. It doesn't seem to be healing properly and she is having a great deal of pain. She's been taking painkillers until she can get back in to see the doctor. We decided to have pizza for supper and, forgetting about the effect of the pain pills, we thought a bottle of wine would be a good compliment to the pizza. Well, the first bottle of wine disappeared so fast that we opened another one. I guess the wine made us feel romantic. But right in the middle of things, the pills and the wine clashed. Betty got upset with me and then any thing else around. Sometimes she sits there like she is now, in another world. At other times she storms around the house like a caged lion, hits me and kicks me. At first I tried holding her tight, but that made her even madder and she kicked me in the groin. Since then, I've been trying to keep away from her until she calms down. My mother happened to call in the middle of one of Betty's rampages and she must have guessed something was wrong."

Just then, as if on cue, Betty jumped to her feet and stormed around the living room uttering oaths and swinging her arms around wildly. She walked into the kitchen and I watched her closely so that she didn't grab a knife and come after Andy and me. Betty came to where Andy was sitting, swore at him and began kicking him with her bare feet. It must have hurt her toes more than Andy's shin, but because of the combination of the pain medication and wine, she felt no pain.

Then I remembered to call Mary. She was relieved to hear my voice and I told her I was all right, but I couldn't tell her everything that was going on. "Honey, I'll be home after a while, don't wait up for me. It may take some time."

By this time Betty had calmed down again and was sitting on the recliner sulking. I tried to speak with her and get her to talk, but she just sat there in a trance. She wouldn't even acknowledge that I was trying to speak with her. Andy sat on the sofa with his hands folded across his chest wondering what to do. He wondered if he had the patience to wait it out.

I, too, wondered how long it was going to take. Thoughts of my bed seemed so far away. Each time it seemed that Betty might be calm enough so that I could leave, she would get agitated and begin her rampage again. I didn't feel comfortable leaving Andy alone with her. She was more reserved in her tirades while I was there.

After a couple of hours, I could see that this could go on all night. I concocted a plan that I thought might work. If Andy and I could get Betty into their car while she was in a relatively calm mood, we could drive to my home. There was a hide-a-way bed in the finished basement where they could sleep. Perhaps the fresh air might help and maybe being in the parsonage would inhibit her outbursts to some extent. After all, her episodes of anger were becoming less frequent and more controlled.

Andy thought the plan was worth a try. He didn't have any other ideas and he was getting tired too. The only one who wasn't getting tired and was still wired was Betty.

I called Mary, who was still awake, to tell her that I was bringing the couple home to spend the night on our hide-a-way downstairs. She didn't say it, but I could hear, "Oh that's just great!" in her voice.

Andy and I waited for the right time when Betty was calm and loaded her into their car. She made the trip to our house without incident. Mary had the hide-a-bed all made up and Betty seemed to be calmer in unfamiliar surroundings. We got the couple settled in for the rest of what was left of the night by around 3 A.M.

At the top of the basement stairs there was a door with a small bolt type lock that wouldn't keep an irritated 5-year-old out. We locked it and settled down in our own bed with the prayer that all would remain quiet downstairs.

Morning came too soon. Mary and I woke without hearing any commotion down below. We got dressed trying not to disturb the couple thinking that they needed their sleep. But as Mary was preparing breakfast, I became concerned because I couldn't hear any activity coming from the basement. Wondering if they were all right, I knocked on the door.

There was no answer.

I knocked again.

There was still no answer.

With some trepidation in my heart, I cautiously opened the door and called, "Andy? Betty?"

Still there was no answer. I crept down the stairs to take a peek. There was no one in the bed but I found a note said, "We have gone home. We couldn't sleep and Betty is doing much better, so we decided to go home. Thank you for your hospitality. We will talk with you later. Thanks again. Andy and Betty."

Later that day Andy called to express their thanks for my coming over to the house, spending all that time with them and bringing them home. He explained that the fresh air and the trip to our home helped Betty recover from the effects of the wine. She was embarrassed about her actions and they talked for a while before deciding to go home where they could sleep better. They were both very appreciative and they learned their lesson about not mixing pain medication with wine.

Not long after, Andy had a job transfer back to his home in Sioux Falls. Now his mother could look out for them. Oh yes, I called her the next morning and explained what had taken place, She was very grateful for what Mary and I had done for her kids.

We saw Andy and Betty in church a couple Sundays before they moved back to Sioux Falls and they seemed happy, very appreciative and still somewhat embarrassed.

That's just one situation a pastor might run into in his ministry. He tries whatever might work. Innovation is a key word. Sometimes it works and sometimes it doesn't. A pastor just has to try like everything depends on him and pray like everything depends on God...because it does.

Chapter 26 – Robbery and Hexes

"Like robbers, they will loot the treasures and leave the temple in ruins." Ezekiel 7: 22

Young people often believe that they know everything when, in reality, they have much to learn and a lot of maturing before them. To try and convince them of this is no easy task. Some have to learn this lesson on their own and often the hard way. Prayer is our strongest weapon to help guide them in the right path.

Our family was about ready to sit down for supper when our son, Scott, came in from playing outside. "Why are those three bikes laying behind the church?" he asked. "It must be some confirmation students who came early."

It was much too early for any students to be at church. It seemed very suspicious so I crossed the alley to the church to investigate. The bikes were not familiar, but as I looked around I noticed that a screen that covered a window that opened into the secretary's office had been pried open. The culprits had to be inside. I opened the back door as quietly as I could so that I might sneak up on whoever was inside. It wasn't quiet enough. I could hear young feet scurrying for the exits and the panic bars on the doors being hit. No one ran past me so I didn't see anyone.

Mary followed me to the church and was standing beside the bikes so they couldn't be used for a getaway. Never the less, one young tough ran past her, hopped on his bike and rode away. Mary considered grabbing him, however, it happened so quickly and he was gone in a flash. It was a good thing she wasn't able to react because the boy would have knocked her down. He wouldn't have cared.

I followed the sound of the one who exited through the front door of the church. As I chased him, a neighbor happened to be driving down the street and saw me pursuing the youth. He timed it just right that when the young boy, who was looking back at me, reached the street he ran into the side of his stopped car. The neighbor hopped out of his vehicle, opened the back door and pushed the youth in. He brought him back to me and I took him into the church office.

Another neighbor, who was watering his lawn, heard the commotion and saw one of the youths fleeing the scene. He chased him in his bare feet far enough to recognize the youth as a boy he had coached in Little League Baseball. He put on his shoes and came over to the church to find out what was happening. He was able to supply the name and address of the boy from his Little League records.

As I dialed the number for the police department, I observed that someone had tried to pry open the safe in the church office. An extra large screwdriver was lying on the floor in the hall.

In a few minutes two police cars arrived. One officer stayed to take a report and question the boy in the office. The other officer left with the name and address of the other boy and to cruise around to see if he could locate the third youth. He returned in a short time with two boys in tow. He found one hiding under a bush a block away. The other boy was hiding at home.

With the three boys together in the church office confessions flowed freely. These thirteen-year-old boys were so scared they were shaking. The police officers recognized all three as having been in trouble with the law before. They confessed to several other church break-ins in the neighborhood. I lectured them about the futility of breaking into churches for money saying, "Most churches don't keep large amounts of money around. Even the offering is counted as soon as possible and deposited in the bank. There is no money in that safe—it contains only important papers. All you have succeeded in doing is to have jammed it so we can't open it with the combination. You have wasted your time and your life in attempting to steal from the Lord's house. If you are truly sorry for your sin, God will forgive you, but you will have to pay for your crimes of robbing the churches of our community. What a shame to waste your young lives on futile activity." The officers led the boys to their cruiser to take them to the Juvenile Detention Center.

Later I went to the three boy's hearing before the judge. My intention was to speak on their behalf. During their questioning at the church office it was clear to me that each boy individually was not bad. It was only when they were together that they were trouble. I wanted to suggest to the judge that, in place of jail time, they be placed in foster homes far away from each other. Two of the boys were living in foster care already and the other boy's home was dysfunctional.

The boys and their lawyers walked past me as I sat on a bench in the hallway and the boys recognized me. I asked the lawyers if I might speak on the boy's behalf. They replied that the boys would have to give their consent. A lawyer returned in a few minutes and told me the boys refused my offer.

I was disappointed that these boys saw me as a threat rather than trying to help them. I did want to help them, but perhaps they were so hardened already that they needed to spend some time in juvenile corrections.

I never saw them again and have no idea how they grew up.

Daniel Rose was a problem teenager of a different nature. He was never in trouble with the law that I know of, but he was flirting with disaster with his Lord. His mother told him in my presence, "I hope that some day you have a child just like you. Then you will understand what I have gone through."

I taught Daniel in confirmation class. He was never interested in learning about his loving Lord who died for him. He fooled around in class and never learned any of his memory work at home. I was uncomfortable confirming him, but I felt holding him back would turn him off to Christ all the more. He had faithful parents who could nurture him in the faith and that was better than my pressuring him.

The week before Confirmation Sunday, I taught the class about Holy Communion and proper preparation for its reception. I stressed that the Bible teaches that it is possible to take communion to one's damnation and the way to guard against that is to make sure your faith is strong.

Evidently Daniel absorbed enough of the teaching to be worried about his reception of communion to his damnation, because on Confirmation Sunday he choked on the wine. I came to realize that it was not surprise at the taste, but genuine fear that he may have taken communion to his own damnation that caused him to choke. He attended church during the following weeks, but he didn't come to the altar with his parents to receive the sacrament.

One Sunday I asked Daniel's mother why he was not attending Holy Communion? She explained her son's fear of condemning himself by receiving it unworthily and that it had grown into an irrational fear of taking communion, period. I went to visit Daniel at home as soon as possible. Armed with the knowledge of his fear I was able to speak to him on terms that he was ready to receive. I knew he was afraid of God's condemnation and that told me that he respected God. We needed to build that respect into faith and trust. He was ready to be taught. The Lord provided the cultivation of Daniel's soul to receive his promise of salvation by faith in Jesus Christ. When I left the house that day, I was reasonably sure that Daniel had the beginning of a saving faith.

This is not to say that everything was perfect in Daniel's walk in faith with his Savior. He refused to attend the youth Bible study on Sunday morning even though his parents and I urged him to go.

He would rather sit in the family car and wait until his parents completed their Bible study. Evidently they were tired of fighting with him about it.

One Sunday after the worship service, as I was greeting the members, Daniel came through the line to shake hands. I thought that I would try a little good-natured teasing to get him to attend the youth class. So, I asked him, "Are you going to attend Bible study today?"

"No, Pastor, I have things to do today."

"What kind of things?"

"Oh, just things."

"I suppose you have homework to do in the car?" I knew he hated homework.

The corners of his mouth turned up into a sly grin that told me he knew I was teasing him. "Not homework. Just things."

Where the idea came from I'll never understand, but I thought I'd try a good-natured threat. "If you don't attend the Bible class today I'll put a hex on you."

Daniel smiled as he turned and walked out the door to the car. No way was he going to attend that Bible class and no idle threat was going to make him!

Around 2:00 P.M. on Monday I received a phone call from Daniel's mother. She reported, "Guess what happened, Pastor! Daniel is in the hospital with a broken leg."

"What happened?"

"He rode his motorcycle to school today. He has been given specific instructions that he may ride it to school and back home and, absolutely, nowhere else. You know Daniel, give him a rule and that's his invitation to break it. He decided he was going to take the cycle for a joy ride during lunch time, and as he turned a corner too fast, it slid on some sand and the bike landed on his leg and it broke. He is feeling sorry for himself and believes his broken leg is God's punishment for disobeying us. Oh, by the way, he thinks you had something to do with the accident because of the hex you placed on him Sunday."

"I'm very sorry that he had the accident, but it is hard for me to believe that he actually thinks that I could really put a hex on him. I'd better get over to the hospital right away."

"Thank you, Pastor. He's in room 324."

I immediately stopped what I was doing and left for the hospital. I ran up the steps to the third floor for the exercise. Daniel's room was down the hall to the right. I knocked on the door as I came around the corner. Daniel looked up from what he was doing and when he saw me fear flashed across his face. He put both hands in front of his eyes in an obvious show that he believed that his plight was a result of the hex I placed on him.

At first I laughed thinking he was returning my teasing of the day before, but as I approached his bed it was obvious he was not laughing. I said, "Daniel, do you really believe that I could put a hex on you?"

"Sure, Pastor! You're a man of God and he'll do whatever you ask."

I realized that there was much more to teach this young man about God. "Daniel," I explained, "God doesn't take orders from me. I am his servant and, anyway, God doesn't give hexes. Hexes are of witchcraft and the devil. God sends us blessings. I was teasing you on Sunday when I said that I would put a hex on you."

Daniel began to relax and I could tell that I had captivated his interest. He didn't give me his undivided attention often, so I decided to take advantage of the situation to teach. "God loves you Daniel. He wants the best for your life and gives you his promise that all that happens to us will work out for our good when we love him and follow his purpose. You are looking for someone else to blame for your broken leg, but it's your responsibility because you disobeyed your parents in riding your motorcycle when they told you not to. We believe that God guides all things, but in your situation, he allowed you to suffer the consequences of your disobedience. Because of your inexperience riding your cycle, you didn't realize that sand on a sharp turn is dangerous. You made the mistake and God allowed the accident to happen so that you might learn the lesson that you are to obey your parents. That lesson comes from a God who loves you and does not punish you. He sent his only Son, Jesus to go to the cross to forgive your sins and to take upon him your punishment.

"But what about the hex you put on me?"

"There was no hex! There was no power behind what I said to you. It was your guilty conscience that made you believe that God was responsible for your accident. In John chapter nine, Jesus and his disciples came upon a man who was born blind. Upon seeing his suffering, Jesus' disciples asked: 'Who sinned, this man or his parents, that he should be born blind?' Jesus answered, 'It was neither that this man sinned, nor his parents, but it was in order that the works of God might be displayed in him.' God is working to bring you closer to him. In John chapter fifteen, Jesus uses the example of a vine, the branches and a vinedresser. The vinedresser is our heavenly Father. Jesus is the Vine and we are the branches.

The Father first "grafts" you to Jesus, the Vine, through his miracle of baptism. Then God prunes away the dead branches of your life in order to produce a more healthy attachment to Jesus. The purpose is so that you will produce more fruit, or dedicated service, in God's kingdom and bring him greater glory."

"You're saying that this happened so that I might grow closer to Jesus and serve him more?"

"That's it exactly! Jesus wants you to be close to him and to trust in him in all situations even when they don't turn out they way you want."

"Wow, he does love me! Why didn't you teach this in confirmation instruction?"

"I did teach that in confirmation, but your heart wasn't open and you didn't listen. I believe the Lord allowed you to have this accident so that your ears and heart would be open to understand. Let's pray that Jesus would enter your heart more fully and that you will grow in his grace and favor." We bowed our heads and prayed together, Daniel and I. It was a time that I had prayed for often, but doubted it would ever come. I learned never to doubt the power of God and the wonderful workings of his ways.

As I left Daniel's hospital room he said, "Thanks, Pastor, for never giving up on me and for your visit. I learned a lot about God's love today and how he cares for me even when I'm in trouble. And I'm in trouble a lot." Daniel made a big turn-around that day. After that he came to church with a smile and started attending the youth Bible study.

He didn't dare skip it anymore.

Chapter 27 – Called to Immanuel

"During the night Paul had a vision of a man of Macedonia standing and begging him, 'Come over and help us.'" Acts 16:9

It seems that when ministers are the most comfortable in a thriving ministry, God sends something to jar us out of complacency and to challenge our ministry gifts. Following six years of blessed ministry at Peace Lutheran Church, I received the call to be senior pastor of Immanuel Lutheran Church in Colorado Springs, Colorado.

It was in the spring of 1977 that the chairman of the Board of Elders from Immanuel telephoned to ask if he could drop by and pay a visit. He was in town and wanted to meet me. I told him that I was happy to meet with him, but that it had to be soon and brief as I was packing and getting ready to go to the airport to fly to St. Louis. Our national church body was having committee meetings over Memorial Day weekend in preparation for a convention to be held in Dallas in July.

Marv Scheefer arrived at my office at church within ten minutes after his telephone call. I was grabbing a few items needed for the meeting in St. Louis. He struck me as a pleasant man of professional bearing with a great love for his Lord. He appeared to be in his mid-forties with dark hair and a strong, handsome face. He mentioned that my name was on the list for consideration for the position of senior pastor at Immanuel Lutheran Church. I was surprised, to say the least. As we visited, it became obvious that he had a great concern for his church in Colorado Springs. I could feel an immediate bond with this man and I liked his easy manner.

I realized that I was under the microscope.

Marv went on to explain, " Immanuel has been vacant in the pastoral office for three years and the congregation is in need of a suitable senior pastor. The previous senior pastor retired after serving the congregation for 34 years. We have been served during the vacancy by a variety of retired pastors. Immanuel is a congregation of about 1,500 souls and 1,000 communing members. The congregation supports a Christian school from kindergarten through the ninth grade. It has 250 students with a principal and vice-principal and 12 teachers. Together with secretaries and other support people the staff numbers 25."

This sounded like a tremendous challenge and a great opportunity. A larger church to serve in a growing city with many opportunities for outreach and ministry was intriguing.

"Marv, I like the idea of a Christian school that our children could attend and grow in their faith together with other Christian children. And I can visualize a very challenging ministry of outreach to the community. I understand that Colorado Springs is a beautiful place to live and raise a family."

" All that is true!" Marv encouraged.

I made up my mind to put myself in the best light so that I would stay in consideration for the call. I gave Marv a brief tour of Peace Church that included the recently completed addition of more seating for the congregation, a large meeting room with a modern kitchen, four classrooms and a library.

Marv understood that my time was limited so he offered to drive me to the airport so we could get better acquainted. This impressed me and I must have made a positive impression on him because I received the call a few weeks later.

My attendance at the convention in July provided an opportunity to visit with many pastors from Colorado and to get their impression of Immanuel congregation. Everyone spoke highly of the church, school and staff. And I was able to meet the principal of the school, Fred Moss, and socialize with him. We enjoyed each others company and that made me even more comfortable about the call.

Arrangements had been made with the congregation's leadership for me to make a stopover to visit in Colorado Springs on my return to Rapid City from Dallas. Two officers from the congregation met me at the airport in Denver and we conversed easily on the 40-minute trip to Colorado Springs. We stopped for lunch at a hotel in the north part of town near the Air Force Academy and the two men made sure that I faced the beautiful spectacle of Pikes Peak.

The faithful members, their organization of my visit, the tour of the church and school and even the question and answer time favorably impressed me with the church leaders.

As the members arrived for the interview session, it was obvious that many of the church leaders were not acquainted with Ed and Harriet who were new members. For as the people entered, they surveyed the group to determine if my wife was present and selected the only face that was unfamiliar. Twice they asked if Harriet, who was a least 20 years my senior, was my wife. Thank goodness she was very youthful for her age and quite attractive.

There were a couple of embarrassing moments for both of us, as we both shook our heads. Ed, however, was enjoying the fact that his wife was mistaken for the wife of the young pastor.

Colorado Springs was beautiful that time of year with Pikes Peak ascending just west of the city all covered in white from an afternoon hailstorm. Even in July the days were comfortable and the evenings cool in the dry mountain air. There were many exciting challenges for ministry in a congregation that was eager for leadership in moving forward for the Lord. I could hardly wait to get home and share my experience with Mary and the children.

During the next couple of weeks plans were made to drive to Colorado Springs with the family so they could get as excited as I was. Marv and his wife, Christine, hosted all of us. Marv entertained our children while Mary and I went about the business of getting acquainted with the church and its members. Two church members who were realtors gave us a tour of the prospective housing market. Moving from the security of a parsonage where everything is provided to ownership would be a huge step. Although housing costs in Colorado Springs were very reasonable and it looked like it would be affordable.

The evening before we were to return to Rapid City, Marv and Christine held a cookout in their back yard for us and all the elders and their wives were invited. After much prayer, I announced my acceptance of the call to be senior pastor of Immanuel Lutheran Church. The leaders were happy that their quest for a new pastor was coming to fulfillment.

But, did they fully understand what they were getting?

We arrived in Colorado Springs the third week of September because I needed to fulfill a commitment to the South Dakota District Lutheran Women's Missionary League.

When we finally arrived in Colorado Springs, we hit the ground running. Members helped us unload the moving truck into a town home we rented from Ed and Harriet until our home was built. The children entered Immanuel School the next day and I was installed in the worship service on Sunday.

The first time the congregation wondered about their new young pastor was on Super Bowl Sunday. The favorite football team of the area was, of course, the Denver Broncos who were playing for the national championship for the first time in their franchise history. Their colors were orange and blue and their mighty defense was nicknamed, "the orange crush." However, it was well known in the congregation that I supported my hometown Minnesota Vikings. As I drove to church that morning, I thought about what I might do to show the people that I would root for the Broncos in the game. It came to me in a stroke of genius. There was a red stole lovingly made by a member of the congregation for use on Reformation Day that was lined with orange material. I could turn it over so that the members could see the orange stole worn over my vestments!

As I entered the sanctuary vested with the orange stole, I was first met with a hush, then a groan and, finally, whispers.

As the service progressed and no one came forward to escort me away to the land of obnoxious preachers, I became more daring. It came time to announce the reading of the Gospel lesson, which should have been: "The Holy Gospel for the first Sunday after Epiphany is…." Instead I said, "The Holy Gospel for the thirteenth Sunday of the Super Bowl is recorded in St. John chapter 1."

I expected a few laughs, but there was only silence.

Deafening silence!

After the service some people complimented me on the orange stole, others thanked me for my support of the Broncos, but most made no mention of it. Either they didn't notice the departure from the appointed color for the day or they didn't think it was worth mentioning.

Some of the more traditional members must have thought to themselves, "T*hat's strike one!*"

As I fished around for a response to the announcement of the Gospel, I found that most didn't even catch my revision. Only those in the choir chuckled, but they were too far away for me to hear.

Not too much later, I was appointed another wife to whom I was not married. Our printer, Harold, had a vision problem. It was uncanny that only occasionally did this cause a problem with his print work. He passed a woman in the dim light of the hallway of the church and greeted her with, "Well, hello Mrs. Grassinger!" It wasn't Mary, but at least she was closer to my age. And thereafter, Harold recognized Jodell as Mrs. Grassinger. Jodell and I shared many laughs about this. She even wanted me to share in claiming her newborn daughter especially when it came time to pay the hospital bill.

I don't think Harold ever did identify the real Mrs. Grassinger.

There was some trepidation in my heart that it might be circulated that I had more than one wife. Oh well, live dangerously!

Was that's strike two?

The next question mark that hung over this new pastor's head came in November. It was time for the annual Immanuel School

Variety Show. A number of the staff and school parents thought it would be great exposure for the new pastor to be involved. It also seemed to be a good way to show my support for the school—so, I reluctantly agreed.

But I didn't know what I was getting into.

They told me I was to be in a skit about three monks. Outside of monks being Catholic, it seemed to be in character.

On the evening of the first rehearsal, I was somewhat concerned that I hadn't been given any script to learn. They told me, "Don't worry. There is no script, only actions."

One of the ladies had sewed a monk's costume for me and had obviously spent a lot of time on it. The brown beanie had curls of yarn sown to it to simulate a monk's hair. The skit was explained to me and it seemed simple enough. We did several runs through until I felt comfortable in what I was to do. That didn't include feeling comfortable about "the pastor" acting that silly in front of church and school parents. One thing I did learn from the rehearsal was that I was going to have to increase the muscle tone in my biceps so that I wouldn't fall flat on my…excuse my French, derriere

The night of the variety show arrived and the school gym was packed with people eager to see what entertainment the committee had come up with. Following the rehearsals, it was determined that the three monks skit would be the biggest hit and was assigned to be the finale. I had to wait the entire show with my jangled nerves.

It was finally time!

The gym was darkened and there was a pause to add suspense. Faintly in the darkness the melody of "The Chapel Bells Were Ringing" began to waft into the gym. Slowly the curtains opened to reveal three ropes suspended from the top of the stage. Dutiful monks dressed in costumes identical to mine were methodically pulling two of the ropes in time to the music. As the music grew louder, a spotlight drew everyone's attention to the center rope that was unattended. I began to make noise and the spotlight darted to the rear of the gym to reveal me, in my monk's costume, running and tripping down the center aisle quite obviously late for the appointed time to ring the bells. I tripped up the steps to the stage, darted to the vacant rope and grabbed hold of it as I skidded past. Assuming a pious demeanor, I began to pull on the bell rope in synchronization with the other two monks as "The Chapel Bells Were Ringing" continued to play. For a few seconds all was in harmony, but then I got a devilish gleam in my eye and began to ring my bell faster than the others. Pretty soon I ran around tangling my rope with the other monks who were trying very hard to keep their bells ringing properly. It was not long before they got caught up in the moment and began to enjoy the devilment. Before long all of the ropes were tangled.

This confusion proceeded for a few moments until the two monks regained their composure, unwound their ropes and returned to their places ringing their bells again in pious synchronization. In the mean time, I had lost hold of my rope and by the time I returned to it, it was about six inches above my reach. In resourcefulness, I found a footstool and dragged it to my rope, but I was still too short to reach it. After a couple of flailing attempts to jump for it, I finally snagged it. But as soon as I reached it, the rope was hoisted so that I was lifted off the stool. I hug there suspended, flailing around until the curtain began to close. Just before the curtain closed completely, the rope was pulled by the stagehands so that it looked like I was being pulled up to the bell tower.

The music stopped, the spotlight went out and there was hysterical laughter and thunderous applause.

I wondered if the members of the congregation would ever take me seriously again.

Was this strike three?

After the show, came my answer. People loved it. They were happy that their new pastor had a sense of humor and could have fun. They were pleased that I was not a stuffed shirt. They learned a lesson that night that Christians don't have to be serious sourpusses but can have fun and laugh together. I was afraid they might be laughing <u>at</u> me and asking themselves "what did we get here? How long can he last?"

That was over 25 years ago. I served Immanuel Congregation all those years until I retired in 2002. And you know what?

They didn't laugh at me.

We laughed together.

And we grew together in our Lord's service, loving Him and rejoicing in His love for us. And we were happy Christians thankful that He sent His only Son to die for us on the cross of Calvary that we might laugh together one day in heaven forever.

Chapter 28 – The Conference in Vail

"Whoever serves me must follow me; and where I am, my servant also will be. My Father will honor the one who serves me." St. John12: 26

It wasn't long before I learned that one of the perks of serving a congregation in Colorado was attending conventions in upscale locations. Our Professional Workers' Conference consisted of pastors, teachers, directors of Christian education and other called church workers and their wives. Most wives wanted to attend the conference to experience the beauty and opulence of places such as Vail, Breckenridge, Snow Mass and Aspen as well as do some shopping. The only drawback was that we could only afford such places during the off-season. Also, the conference planners realized that if there was snow on the mountains attendance at the conference sessions would be slim. These three-day meeting were fun to attend and a great temporary getaway, but they could never replace the joy and blessing of a vibrant and fulfilling ministry.

The first Worker's Conference I attended was in the fascinating and beautifully designed ski village of Vail. The conference center was the Lion's Head Lodge and the participants stayed in ski condos.

Part of the fun of the conference this year was the trip up to Vail. Immanuel congregation had just purchased a pre-owned Greyhound bus with a rebuilt engine, plush interior and fresh paint on the exterior with the lettering, "Immanuel Lutheran Church and School" emblazoned on the sides. We were so proud of that bus and eager to take it on our maiden voyage. It looked so impressive. It's too bad it seldom ran as impressively as it looked.

The bus driver calculated that the travel time from Colorado Springs to Vail would take longer in the bus than driving by car. We expected that the bus would chug up the mountain passes slowly, but anticipated that we could roll freely down the other side of the pass making up the lost time. We also had made arrangements to stop in Denver to pick up the members of another church staff and that added another half-hour to our schedule.

The trip was enjoyable as we were able to socialize on the bus. Conversation grew even louder after we picked up the other staff. But then we entered the mountains on Interstate 70. The chugging up the pass was slower than expected. An assistant bus driver picked up the manual and read how to break in the new engine. He read out loud to the driver, "During the first 500 miles the RPM's of the engine must never be allowed to exceed 2,000." This posed an immediate problem as we crested the pass and started down the other side. The engine RPM's quickly wound up to 2,000 and the bus was only traveling 30 miles an hour. In order to keep the RPM's under the required limit, the driver had to shift into second gear and we crawled down the pass. So the bus with its passengers chugged slowly up the pass and slowly down the pass at least twenty times in the 70 miles to Vail. Needles to say, our estimated time was thrown way off and we arrived in Vail late.

Never the less, undaunted, we piled out of the bus, unpacked our luggage and checked into our condo units. They were beautifully decorated and spacious. Most units had views of the ski slopes with their lifts.

I uttered a prayer for snow. God answered, "No!"

One example of the close relationship between the members of our staff was shown by the tradition of sharing a great turkey feast. Tuesday evening was reserved for the big dinner. The ladies would place the pre-prepared turkey in the oven as soon as we checked into our condos. Everyone in our group pitched in by either preparing their favorite dish or, in the case of some of the men, provided the fixings, rolls or condiments. This was the first time that I had the pleasure of observing the organization of so many in preparing such a tasty dinner.

The conference was interesting and inspiring, meeting with friends was a joy and the turkey dinner on Tuesday evening was a special delight as we enjoyed the fellowship of a caring staff

There was maturity and a wealth of experience in the ranks of this dedicated group of people. They were innovative and successful in their efforts for the advancement of Christian education in our school as well as in the larger setting of the district. While most of the other church staffs fragmented at these conferences, the Immanuel staff stuck together and functioned as a group. This caused some jealousy among those at the meeting.

Wednesday evening was scheduled to be the banquet for the entire conference. A large room was set with tables and the finest tableware for the great occasion. As a prelude to the banquet, our staff and a few others were invited to a social time at the condo of the director of Lutheran Valley Retreat. I'm afraid that we all socialized too long and arrived at the banquet late. Evidently the word of where we had been had gotten out and there was some animosity about us being singled out for the social.

Our group arrived at the entrance to the banquet room and gazed at everyone else seated around all of the available tables.

There was no room left for the Immauel staff!

Those who were seated gradually grasped the gravity of the situation, but instead of being sympathetic, a cynical laugh began to permeate the floor. Someone even had the audacity to say, "Poor Immanuel! They've been partying too long and now there's no place for them to sit."

But wait!

The Lion's Head waiters grasped the situation and began to set tables, of all places, on a terrace that placed us on a loftier level above everyone else. When those below caught on, an audible groan was heard that communicated that the staff at Immanuel had received preferential treatment again.

By the time the tables were set and we were being seated, everyone below us was enjoying their chicken dinner. A waiter announced to us that the kitchen had run out of chicken. Someone on the floor overheard the waiter and again the word was being circulated in a tittering way, "They ran out of food for Immanuel!"

The waiter continued so only we could hear, "Don't worry. The chef will come up with something for you all."

Time flashed by and the waiters brought out our salad followed by plate after plate of sirloin steak, baked potatoes, and vegetable medley and set them before us with great flair. Silence enveloped those down below as they observed what we were being served and many just looked in disgust at their chicken bones thinking, *The Immanuel staff had pulled it off again! Those lucky dogs!*

What happened that evening wasn't luck. It was the fulfillment of Jesus' advice in the Parable of the Wedding Guest recorded by St. Luke in the 14th chapter, "When you are invited to a feast, take the lowest place, so when your host comes, he will say to you, 'Friend, move up to a better place.' Then you will be honored in the presence of all your fellow guests. For everyone who exalts himself will be humbled, and he who humbles himself will be exalted."

We served our Lord humbly because we loved Jesus, not for human honor. So, we were not being pretentious at the banquet that evening, but God honored us in the presence of our fellow guests. The rewards and accolades that came to us were the result of hard work and a dedication to serve our Lord to the fullest.

That singleness of purpose and love for our Lord was what united us.

Chapter 29 - Good Communication is Important

"I pray that you may be active in communicating your faith, so that you will have a full understanding of every good thing we have in Christ." Philemon 6

Like a good marriage, positive communication between staff and among members is very important. It is like a reporter checking his sources before going to print. The savvy pastor will not jump to conclusions based on hearing one side of an issue. That wisdom was quickly brought to mind again early in my ministry at Immanuel.

It seemed like communication could get really fowled up at the church. Perhaps it was because the congregation was so large and the staff so big that there were many more mouths to go through. I was constantly double-checking the accuracy of information that came to me.

One situation got away from me because of the press for time to begin a Sunday morning worship service. It was less than five minutes before the service was to begin. My associate, Pastor Jerry Dollar picked up the phone that was urgently complaining to be to be answered. I was in another part of the building, so I didn't hear the conversation. By the time he came to me with the information, it was three minutes before service time.

He relayed the conversation to me, "Barb Anderson just called and she wants a prayer of comfort for someone whose daughter died suddenly. The name sounded like… Rona Finley or something like that."

I thought for a moment mulling over the names in the congregation who had daughters that sounded like Finley. "Was it Fridley? Rhonda Fridley?"

"Ya, that's it!"

"Wow! Rhonda is young, like in her 30's. That's so sad. I'll put her mom on the prayer list for comfort."

The service progressed to the time for the prayers and as I included the prayer of comfort for Mrs. Fridley, there was an audible gasp from two of her friends sitting in the congregation. They told me later that they were so shocked that they couldn't wait for the service to get over so they could go over to her home and comfort her. In fact, they left before the announcements.

Within minutes, the two friends were ringing the doorbell at Mrs. Fridley's. She answered the door with, "What a pleasant surprise! Come on in and have a seat on the sofa. I'll go put the coffee pot on." And she disappeared into the kitchen before the ladies could say a word to her. One lady turned to the other and whispered, "She doesn't seem upset at all for just having lost her daughter!" "I couldn't be that cheery if my daughter had died!" said the other.

Just then the toilet flushed in the bathroom, the door opened and out popped Rhonda fresh out of the shower with a bathrobe on and a towel wrapped around her hair.

The women on the sofa came close to having a heart attack when they saw Rhonda. They jumped out of the sofa and ran to hug her. Then they called to Mrs. Fridley in the kitchen and told her what they heard in church.

They could now really enjoy their coffee with Mrs. Fridley and had a good laugh about the error in communication. Mrs. Fridley said, "She was glad that it was a mistake." And so did Rhonda. The ladies promised to call me as soon as they got home and straighten out the confusion.

By this time, things had been clarified on my end. Rhonda Ridgley, who was not a member, had called back to make plans for the funeral of her aged aunt Rhoda, who died during the night.

The mix up wasn't Pastor Jerry's fault or anyone else's. It was just one of those situations that happens when under pressure and in a rush. But we agreed that, in the future, we would get the message clearly on the phone and write it down or no prayer would be offered. It would be much better not to offer a prayer than to pray someone to death.

Another under pressure situation arose shortly before a church service a few weeks later. Pastor Jerry had mentioned to me, off handedly, that if he was not at church by 20 minutes before the service on a Sunday on which he was to preach, to call him. It was now 7:45 and I hadn't seen Jerry come in. Somewhat in a panic, I quickly dialed his number. A young voice answered that sounded like his son. "Jon? Is your father out of bed?"

"No! He's still sleeping."

"Well, hurry and get him up! He's supposed to preach today!"

At the same time as I hung up the phone, the door opened and in came Jon and Pastor Jerry. Jerry explained that there was an accident blocking traffic that held them up.

Then it dawned on me that somewhere in Colorado Springs was a boy named Jon who was shaking his father awake yelling,

"Dad, Dad, the pastor just called and said you have to get up! You're preaching today!"

I'm glad that I didn't identify who I was.

We laughed at the situation and learned another important lesson. Be careful how you dial.

I again learned about clear communication with members when I visited Margaret Sennert in the hospital. Margaret had just delivered a baby a couple of weeks earlier and I was curious as to why she was back in the hospital. As I stood at the foot of her bed, she tried to explain that she got an abscess on her breast from nursing the baby. She could see from my expression, that I did not fully comprehend her. So she said, "Come here and I will show you." I began to back up uncertain of what I might see. Margaret laughed and said, "I was going to draw you a picture."

"Oh!"

Then I came forward sheepishly relieved and I understood much better after she drew me the picture. She was a pretty good artist; good enough so that I still blushed a little when I looked at her drawing.

Everyone needs to work on their communication skills and understanding one another at work, in marriage, in sports and in all of life. Ministers of the Gospel also need to work on their own communication skills daily.

Immanuel Lutheran Church of Colorado Springs

Chapter 30 – Why Lord, Why?

"Dear friends, do not be surprised at the painful trial you are suffering, as though something strange were happening to you." I Peter 4: 12

Sometimes horrible things happen to Christians and there is no simple answer to the question, "Why?" The words from Romans 8:28 are comforting, "And we know that in all things God works for the good of those who love him, who have been called according to his purpose." But it requires a mountain of faith from a Christian to console someone at the time of a tragic and unnecessary loss of a loved one. The question must be answered by a strong faith and trust that God works all things for the good of those who love Him.

Max Malarkey was a family man and a Christian that attended our church. He was married to a plucky redheaded German gal named Marge whom he had met in Germany while serving in the military. Marge had been an Olympic swimmer in Deutschland. They had three grown daughters. Marge's mother lived with them and we called her, Oma, the German name for grandma. They lived in a middle class, immaculate home on a residential street right out of Better Homes and Gardens.

Max had worked at a variety of jobs in the past, but now was a security guard for a bingo parlor that was frequented during the day by seniors. One of his responsibilities was to deposit the morning receipts in the bank, then he would drive home for a quick lunch and return to work for the afternoon session.

On this bright, sunny day Max made the deposit at the bank and was heading home likely with carefree thoughts of lunch. He was crossing a busy intersection at the corner of Academy Boulevard and Airport Road when a sedan crashed into the driver's side of his pickup truck.

I received the call at church from Max's youngest daughter, "Pastor, Dad's been seriously injured in an accident and he's in the emergency room of Memorial Hospital! Can you come right away?"

"Of course! I'll be there as soon as I can."

When I arrived, Sandy was in the ER waiting room. Visibly shaken and crying she told me, "Dad didn't make it. The doctor told me that he died on impact. Pastor, he didn't suffer and probably didn't even know what hit him."

I held Sandy's hand as we sat together and she relayed what the police had told her.

"Dad was on his way home for lunch when a car ran the red light and crashed into his pickup. The car was carrying four young men in their twenties who were drunk. The driver was also high on drugs and he only suffered a leg injury. The car was a rental and the trunk was full of drugs and drug paraphernalia. Dad didn't have a chance!" She fell into my arms crying.

We prayed together for comfort from God and for consolation in the tragedy that would envelope the family.

"Sandy," I said gently, "Does your mother know?"

"No! She's house sitting at Kissing Camels and I don't want to break the news to her over the phone."

"Do you know the address? I'll go over to the house and tell her. Do you want to go with me?"

"No, I better go home and tell Oma. She's expecting Dad for lunch and would be worried by now."

Suddenly there was a great commotion at the entrance to the ER. Two paramedics and two policemen were wheeling in a patient who was cursing and swearing. I noticed that he had a badly injured leg. He was strapped tightly to the gurney and was yelling, "You can't keep me! There's nothing wrong with my leg! I don't want to go to the hospital! I didn't do anything wrong! The other guy ran into me!"

It was obvious that he was "out of it."

I realized that this was the driver of the car that ran into Max. I pitied him because of the trouble he was in and because he was so "out of it" that he didn't understand what had happened.

I easily found the house where Marge was sitting and rang the doorbell.

"Pastor! How? Why are <u>you</u> here?" she questioned with a furrowed brow.

"Marge, please let me come in and we'll sit down."

"There's been an accident, hasn't there? It must be Max! Is he alright?"

"Marge, Max was involved in a terrible accident. And, I'm sorry to have to tell you this, but Max died. He was taken to heaven immediately upon impact and probably didn't even know what hit him."

I held Marge in my arms for a long time as she sobbed. Finally she asked, "What happened?"

I explained.

We prayed for our Lord's comfort and the reassurance to concentrate on Max's victory in heaven and gave thanks that he suffered no pain.

Marge felt she could not leave her house-sitting job, but asked if I would arrange it so Sandy and Oma could come there?

I called their home and Sandy had just finished telling Oma what happened. Sandy said she would bring Oma right over so that they could all be together.

When they arrived, we prayed together and read scripture promises of heaven for those who believe in Jesus. It was comforting for the family, but the lingering question remained, "Why did Jesus take Max home now?"

It is humanly impossible to understand the mind of God and I'm glad, or he would be like me and that's a scary thought. We can come up with human possibilities, but they are probably way off.

Max had been diagnosed with the beginning stages of Alzheimer's. Maybe God wanted to take him to heaven to prevent him from having to endure the progression of the disease. We don't know, but we still look for answers that will satisfy our human questioning.

A few mortal answers satisfy…most don't.

The most fulfilling answer to the question of, "Why" is for us to stand at the foot of our Savior's cross. Then look to him and his great love and trust in his promise, "God works for good to those who love him…" Then we must stop asking, "Why?" and turn in thanks and praise to God for his great love, mercy and gift of heaven. The more completely we focus on our victory in heaven and of being forever reunited, the more comfort we will feel.

Not that it is easy to lose a loved one.

It's not!

Chapter 31 – Kiss the Girl and Make Her What?

"Even in laughter the heart may ache, and joy may end in grief." Proverbs 14:13

Often situations are beyond our control, but as Christians we trust that our Lord knows all things and guides all things. This is comforting for a minister of the Lord when he knows there is nothing he can do. We can trust in the Lord, yet we can laugh as we realize that God has a wonderful sense of humor.

John Spangler called to inform the church office that his wife, Paula, was undergoing surgery and asked if I would visit her later that morning. He left the room number at Penrose Hospital with the secretary.

About 11 A.M. I headed to the hospital figuring the surgery would be over and Paula would be out of recovery. It was a beautiful summer day in Colorado. A light, cooling breeze brushed my cheeks as I walked from the car to the hospital entrance. Since I knew the room number, I took the elevator directly to the 9th floor and proceeded to room 912. Knocking as I entered I was surprised to find that it wasn't Paula in the bed.

This lady was sound asleep.

Backing out of the room so I didn't disturb the sleeping patient, I headed to the nurse's station to find out where Paula was. "Oh, while she was in surgery we put someone else in that room," explained the nurse. "Mrs. Spangler is two rooms down the hall in 916."

Backtracking down the hall, I found room 916 and knocked on the door. This time a cheery voice said, "Come in!" Paula was sitting up in bed looking bright and fresh, not like someone who had just come out of surgery. We visited a while about her surgery and recovery. I gave a devotion and prayer for her recovery. Then she asked, "How did you know I was having surgery?"

"John called the office to notify me."

"Do you know where he is?"

I detected a little hostility in her voice. "No, hasn't he been here?"

She poured out her story. "John brought me to the hospital early this morning. He stayed with me until I was taken into surgery. He told me that rather than hanging around the waiting room, he would go and finish a painting job. He told me he would be back by the time I came out of surgery. I haven't seen him since." I sensed Paula's worry and aggravation about John's whereabouts. It was hard to tell which emotion was stronger.

Thinking I could go over to John's painting location and check on him, I asked Paula, "Do you know where John is working?"

"No, I have no idea."

"Does he have a cell phone?" This was before cell phones were prevalent.

"No!"

"I'm sure he was just delayed. He probably got tied up talking with someone. You know how John loves to talk. He'll be by after a while. If he doesn't show up by this afternoon, call me."

As I drove back to church I wondered, *this wasn't like John. He was devoted to his wife. If he said he would be back at a certain time, he would be. Something wasn't right!* However, as I pulled into the church parking lot, there was John's truck parked by the entrance to the office. I went in.

John was visiting with Jo Ann, my secretary, without a care in the world. "Hi John! I'm surprised to find you here. I just came from the hospital visiting Paula. She is wondering where you are and she is a bit worried." I decided not to tell him he was in a little trouble with her too.

"Well, Pastor," John drawled. "I went back to the hospital after finishing a half hour job and went up to her room. Paula was sound asleep. I sat for a while and waited for her to wake up, but she slept on. I decided I'd run over to church and pick up some things and run right back. So I gave her a kiss on the cheek and noticed that she didn't look so good. Then I stopped to visit with Jo Ann for a while."

"That's odd. When I saw her, she was sitting up in bed and looked very well."

"Humm! Strange. I'd better get back there or she'll be a little ticked."

"She is already on the verge," I warned. "By the way, you know she is in room 916."

"No! She is in room 912."

"That room has another lady in it. I stopped there first and recognized it wasn't Paula. The nurse told me she was moved to room 916 down the hall."

"Oh! Oh!" said John sheepishly. "I was in the wrong room! No wonder the lady in that bed didn't look so good. She wasn't my wife…and I kissed her!"

"You'd better get back to the hospital fast and do some swift explaining."

Without another word, John left.

The next afternoon, I stopped by the hospital to visit Paula. John was dutifully sitting in a chair next to her bed.

They were holding hands.

We laughed together as we reviewed the previous days activities. "I just can't let John out of my sight for a moment," Paula said teasingly. "He'll go around kissing other women when I'm laid up."

"I sure didn't mean too," laughed John. "It was a good thing that lady in 912 didn't wake up while I was kissing her or I could be in real trouble!"

The Grassinger family at the celebration of Pastor Tim's 25th Anniversary in the ministry.

Chapter 32 – Tomorrow Will Be Better

"Why are you downcast, O my soul? Why so disturbed within me? Put your hope in God, for I will praise him, my Savior and my God." Psalm 42:5

Suicide is always a tragic situation. It is doubly tragic when the victim is a youth. A police officer I knew happened to be investigating the suicide of a young man from our congregation. His take on it was, "It is so very sad that these young people get so depressed that they think nothing will get better. If they would wait one day usually things change for the better."

It was a sunny Saturday afternoon when the call came to our home. It was Tim LaFay on the phone and he was distressed. "Pastor, Clark returned home from being with his buddies and found Chance dead. It looks like suicide. Can you come right away?"

"I'll be there just as soon as I can."

Mary asked, "Do you want me to go along?"

"Honey, I'm always glad to have you come with me. It might be pretty gory in the house, but you don't have to go in." We both jumped into the car and headed for the LaFay's.

When we arrived, Clark who was Chance's younger brother by a couple years was sitting on the front step looking miserable. The police were there and the coroner was zipping up the body bag getting ready to put Chance on the gurney to take him out to his vehicle.

We talked to Clark and asked what had happened? He told us that he had asked Chance to go with him to the movies with his friends, but Chance was tired from working at the Antler's Hotel. He wanted to stay home and watch television. When Clark got home the television was on and Chance was slumped in the chair, his revolver was in his right hand and blood was splattered over the wall.

"Dad's inside," he said.

I went in to comfort Tim. Mary stayed outside with Clark.

The body had been removed and I was thankful for that. There was a lot of blood on the wall and on the floor next to the chair. Tim was sitting at the kitchen table with his head in his hands. He was shaking his head and crying, "Why? Why did he do it?"

I sat down at the table with Tim and put my hand on his shoulder. "Tim, it's a question we may never have the answer for. Do you have any clues? Had Chance been depressed?"

"He seemed alright. Everything was good with his girlfriend. Chance did complain about the behavior of some of the boys staying at the Antler's for the President's Hockey Tournament. He told me that the hotel was full of boys from the age of eight to sixteen who were running up and down the halls yelling, making messes and being obnoxious. It was Chance's job to keep order, but he couldn't gain control. The boys had no supervision and were very disrespectful to Chance, but I wouldn't expect something like that to bring him to do something like this."

"One, often, can never come to fully understand what was going on in the mind of someone who commits suicide. It's usually a mystery."

A police officer entered the house and said he needed to interview Clark because he was the one who found the body. Tim said it was all right. I said, "I would like to be present during the interview to support Clark " The officer said that it would be helpful to have me there to serve as a witness.

The officer grilled Clark about why he came home when he did, how he found the body and if he had ever touched the gun. He was making sure that Clark was in no way responsible for his brother's death. The questions seemed harsh at the time, but Clark's story held true to the facts. He was somewhat upset with the line of questioning, but he knew that it had to be done and he had nothing to hide. He was grateful that I was with him.

Fran, Chance's mother, was on a day trip with some friends who traveled to a sightseeing location once a month. Tim tried to reach her but it was impossible. It was probably better that way. She was due to arrive home soon and I dreaded it because I knew that she would take it very hard and possibly get hysterical.

She surprised me. Fran did take the bad news very hard and cried, "Chance. Oh my Chance!" That was to be expected, but she was not hysterical. It was obvious that this family's faith was holding them together. We said many prayers together that God would give them comfort and strength in the face of this tragedy. Fran prayed, "Help me to understand why Chance did this." Clear answers to her prayer were not forthcoming.

Funerals for a suicide are difficult. A pastor must choose his words carefully. While wanting to give the utmost comfort, he can't answer all questions. We believe that God works all things for our good, but in a case like this, a person has taken maters into his own hands. We can still look for the good that God can bring out of all situations.

The family thanked me for a comforting funeral service and message, but reassurance of God's love and the victory of heaven for all who believe were just the beginning.

Fran required the most ongoing care and reassurance. She died prematurely four years later from an illness complicated by her broken heart. Tim and Clark are successfully struggling on in life. It is a burdensome sadness they will carry all their life and it didn't have to be.

Chapter 33 – Headed for the Funny Farm

"Do not let your hearts be troubled. Trust in God; trust also in me." St. John 14:1

The image of a servant of the Lord is to be closely protected from being tarnished. However, appearances may be deceiving at times. This was one of those times.

Our church had just completed an extensive renovation of the facilities. It consisted of asbestos removal for carcinogenic precautions, renovation of a large meeting room, enlarging the secretary's office and separation of the senior pastor's office into two offices. A large section of the church appeared brand new.

The day the furniture was moved from the temporary module back into the church was shaping up to be very busy. My office needed a lot of organization and some homey decorating to make it look presentable. Mary came with me that morning because she has an excellent eye for decorating and hanging pictures.

Everything moved along smoothly in the morning. Pictures were hung, books put on the shelves and furniture arranged. It was beginning to look like an inviting pastor's office, at least one where I could work comfortably.

We took a break for lunch and then things became rushed. The funeral was scheduled for 2:00 P.M. I reviewed my funeral sermon prepared the day before, checked the order of the service and was putting on my robe when the phone rang. A member demanded some information right at that moment. I told him that I was to conduct a funeral in 15 minutes and I would get back later with the requested information. The individual made it clear that he was not happy that I made the funeral a priority ahead of him and he hung up.

The phone rang again and a young lady wanted to set her wedding date and to begin the marriage counseling. I told her I had a funeral in 10 minutes and I would get back to her later. She hung up indignantly. I had the feeling she thought I was lying so I could put her off.

While this was going on, Mary was crawling on her hands and knees applying scratch remover to my desk.

Before the phone could ring again, I asked my secretary to hold all calls. It was while I was talking to her on the intercom that a dignified white haired man snuck past my ever-protecting secretary and appeared at my office door. He was tastefully dressed in a gray suit and loomed in the doorway about six foot four. He began to speak while I was still on the phone. "Where do you want me to have the musical combo set up?"

I hung up the phone and glanced at my watch. It was seven minutes until two. "Musical combo?" I asked incredulously. "I don't know anything about a combo!" I pictured longhaired musicians in jeans and t-shirts with garish emblems carrying a guitar, accordion, tambourine and a set of drums. How else would you picture a musical combo?

He said, "You have to let them play! They came all the way from Pueblo for the funeral."

"Who asked them to play?"

"The deceased's brother, Les Kuhlman. The group has a long-time friendship with the family."

All this time, Mary had been hidden from the tall man's view by my desk. She was still busy on her hands and knees polishing in the kneehole. I glanced down in time to notice that she was finished with that area and ready to come around the corner into the man's view. I wanted to will her to stay where she was. I hoped she was listening to the conversation and might realize how it would look for her to come peeking out from behind my desk. My mind froze on the Monica Lewinsky and President Clinton indiscretion that was fresh in everyone's mind.

Mary had been too busy polishing to even be aware of the man's presence. She thought I was still talking on the telephone. As she poked her head around the corner, the man looked down at her and his eyebrow raised just a little. I could read his mind and it wasn't good. My robe was partially thrown over one arm.

I didn't try to explain. That may have made the situation look even worse but I didn't care. I didn't have time. I asked the man, "Where's the combo? I'll have to check and see what this is all about."

"They are in the balcony."

I rushed past him completing my robe application and left him staring down at my wife on her hands and knees.

Upon reaching the balcony, I breathed a sigh of relief. Part of it may have been catching my breath. The musical combo was a chamber music group consisting of violin, harp and cello. The musicians were two ladies and a man dressed in appropriate black formal attire.

I heaved a big sigh of relief.

"John," I said to the organist who had been playing pre-service music for some time, "Work in this musical group with a pre-service piece and one during the service and let them play after the service. I didn't know they were coming and I apologize for the last minute confusion." John being a great person and easy to work with said, "That's fine with me."

It was time for the service to begin, but the family was late. Fortunately this provided an opportunity for the "combo" to play a selection and it sounded wonderfully professional. It also gave me a chance to catch my breath, get reorganized, put on the wireless microphone and check it. I thought of Mary and the man in my office and wondered if there was any conversation or explanation going on. I didn't care—didn't have time.

Just then the front door opened and the family came streaming in led by brother Les. I called him over to the side and asked, "Why didn't you tell me about the musical group coming from Pueblo?"

"I'm sorry Pastor, they called this morning to say they could come and I thought you could work them in."

"It would have been less stressful if I would have had some advanced warning. We worked them in at the last moment and everything will be fine, but for a while there I was so stressed that I felt like I could go to the funny farm!"

At that moment an usher came from the church and reported, "Pastor, your microphone is turned on and you're broadcasting everything you're saying in the church."

Talk about being stressed! This harried minister, who had just announced to everyone over the P.A. system that he felt like he could go to the funny farm, was going to have to lead a solemn funeral service and preach that we are to trust in God at all times.

After a prayer with the family, I led the procession down the center aisle. When I arrived at the front of the church I didn't want to turn around and face everyone, but I had to or the service wouldn't get started. It wasn't as bad as I expected. There were a few smiles, but most, I think, understood.

No one even mentioned it. Maybe they were afraid they might push me over the edge to that funny farm.

The funeral proceeded without a hitch.

Mary told me later that she never said a word to the man. He shrugged his shoulders and disappeared down the hall.

Several years after the funeral, Les was suffering the effects of cancer. He battled it at home as long as he was able, but it had progressed to the point that he needed specialized care. His family checked him into an inpatient hospice facility across the street from the church. I visited him there.

Les received the best of care at hospice, but he would do anything to go home. He prayed for it, he tried bribing the nurses and he would have called a cab if he had a phone.

I went to visit Les one day after he had been there for a couple weeks. As I entered his room he seemed to have a different gleam in his eye. He asked, "Did they tell you at the nurses station, what I did?" I replied, "No, why? What have you been up to?"

He started to explain. A nurse came into the room, but Les continued as proud as he could be of the antic he was revealing.

"My son Tony, you know Pastor the oldest one who is a fireman, came to see me a couple days ago. I begged him to take me home. Well, he promised to take me if I could get downstairs to the entrance by myself. He believed that I was too weak to get there and that would settle it. I thought that I would show him. So, two nights ago, I waited for the floor to become quiet and the nurses to be busy elsewhere. I crawled out of bed, climbed into my wheel chair and snuck through the hall to the elevator. I was already pretty pooped by the time I got there, but I pushed the down button anyway. When I reached the main floor I pulled myself along by holding onto the railings. It took all the effort I could muster. Finally I made it to the entrance, but once I was there, I realized there was no way I could prove to Tony that I had made it. I saw the fire alarm on the wall and knew that if I pulled it Tony would get the word. I didn't realize that by pulling it I would put the whole building into panic and lockdown and cause so much commotion. The fire truck and paramedics arrived simultaneously with sirens blaring. The jig was up because two nurses spotted me. It was a good thing they showed up because I was too exhausted to get back to my room by myself. I was in a lot of trouble with the firemen and got a lecture from them. They recognized me as Tony's dad and said I should know better. But what could they do to me? I was dying anyway."

"That's quite a caper, Les. You sure showed Tony. So why are you still here?"

"That's just it, Pastor. Tony said that I didn't walk to the entrance, so it didn't count."

We laughed together and even cried some.

Les died two weeks later and I presided at his funeral. I didn't have to worry about last minute surprises or musical combos because his wife was in charge of the arrangements. But I won't forget Les for his extemporization and determination.

Chapter 34 – The Funeral That Never Happened

"Where, O death, is your victory? Where, O death, is your sting? The sting of death is sin, and the power of sin is the law. But thanks be to God! He gives us the victory through our Lord Jesus Christ." I Corinthians 15:57

Some situations are so unusual that no one has ever considered devising a process to deal with them. That was the case with the death and funeral of Phil Holms.

It was the first Wednesday in Advent and a worship service was scheduled at Immanuel for 7 P.M. Mary and I were just sitting down for supper about 5 P.M. when the telephone rang. It was Frieda Holms on the other end of the line. I knew something had to be amiss because she had never called me in 25 years.

Frieda began conversationally, "Hello Pastor. How are you today? Am I interrupting your mealtime? I can call back if you are busy."

"That's alright, Frieda," I told her, still feeling uneasy about her call knowing there must be more of a problem than she was letting on. "How may I help you?"

Frieda began to pour out more than I wanted to hear. "Phil died last night!"

"Oh Frieda, I'm so sorry to hear that! Has he been sick or in the hospital?"

"Oh no, he died at home. I just came back from talking to the neighbor lady and I told her about Phil dying. She asked me if I had called anyone and I told her no. She thought I should tell someone and so I called you. I hope you don't mind."

"Of course not, Frieda I'm happy that you called me but I'm so sorry for your loss. Phil was such a wonderful man and you two were so happy together. You'll miss him greatly." Since Phil died during the night and it was now five in the evening, I figured that Frieda must have contacted the funeral home by now, so I asked, "Have you made any funeral arrangements and what funeral home have you chosen?"

"That's just it, Pastor, I don't know who to call. Would you suggest the name of a good funeral home?"

"Frieda, where is Phil now?"

"He's lying here on the floor in the living room."

"He's where?"

"He's lying here in the living room next to me. He has been acting strange lately. He went to bed early last night, but he couldn't sleep. He got out of bed and went into the living room and sat down on the floor. He was hallucinating that he was shipwrecked on a deserted island. He pulled all the cushions off the sofa and chairs and gathered them around him. Then he tipped over the coffee table and arranged everything into the shape of a boat. I think he believed it was his life raft. He sat there breathing very hard until he suddenly grabbed his chest, tried to pull himself up by the drapes, let out a cry and slumped over. I listened for his breathing, but he was dead."

"Did you call 911 or the paramedics?"

"No. There was no need of that. I knew he was gone."

"Frieda, just hold tight. I'll be there as soon as I can." I was familiar enough with the procedure for deaths at home to know that the police had to be called. I dialed the number for the police dispatcher and told her the situation and that I would meet the officers at the Holms home.

Mary offered to go with me to the house. I grabbed the things that I would need for the Advent worship service, as I had no idea how long this would take. As we drove to the Holms', I filled Mary in on the details of the phone call and I reflected on the facts I knew about this loving couple. Phil, who was an African-American serviceman, met Frieda during the United States occupation of Germany following World War II. They fell in love and were married in Germany. After Phil's tour was over, he brought his new bride to America. Tearfully, Frieda left her family behind in Germany and came to her new country to begin a new chapter in her life. In those days it wasn't easy to be a German war bride and a couple with mixed racial backgrounds. But they applied themselves to hard work and minded their own business and America was good to them. They had a son, Willy, who was now married and living in Denver. He was a truck driver. Phil had been retired from maintenance work for ten years. The couple was inseparable and they made a handsome pair. Phil was over six-foot tall and good-looking with black hair that was graying at the temples. He walked straight because of his military bearing and stood much taller than Frieda, who was about five-foot five and a little on the stout side. She had a pretty smile and eyes that flashed with the excitement of life and all that it had to offer. She was grateful for her life because she had survived the allies bombing of her home in Germany while some of her family perished.

I remembered the time she was interviewed by a newspaper reporter following a worship service at church on May 8th about her experiences during World War II. It was on the fiftieth anniversary of VE Day and the reporter came to our church because someone told her we were the "German Lutheran Church." As Frieda related her story of the nightly bombings, death and devastation upon her family, the reporter broke down and cried. When she regained her composure she said to me, "I have never heard a more tragic, sad story in my life."

Phil and Frieda attended church faithfully until their legs became too weak to support them. Age was taking its toll.

It seemed like an eternity before we arrived at the couple's modest home. When we finally pulled up, two police cruisers were already parked in front. Mary and I entered the front gate and ran up the steep flight of stairs to the front door. It was open and we could see the officers inside evaluating the scene. As we entered the house, I introduced Mary and myself to the police officers as Frieda and Phil's pastor.

Both officers appeared genuinely puzzled. One of the officers was scratching his head. He came over to me and asked, "How familiar are you with this couple?"

"I have known them for over twenty years."

The officer appeared relieved as he continued, "What can you tell us about them? The fact that the living room looks like a fight took place, the curtains have been pulled out of the wall and his body has been here so long looks very unusual. It has all the makings of a crime scene."

I could understand how it looked to them. Everything was as Frieda described over the phone plus some things she left out. Phil was lying on the floor naked and the curtains that he grabbed had, fortunately, draped his body granting him some dignity. He was still in remarkable shape for a man of 78. Mary joined Frieda who was sitting at a kitchen table. She began to comfort her.

I continued, "I'm the one who put in the call to the police. Frieda called me at about 5 P.M. and told me what happened." I related to the officer what she had told me. The other policeman moved within earshot. I completed my account by saying, "I know this couple well enough to be certain that nothing clandestine has happened here. Phil has been having hallucinations for a couple months and his heart has not been good for some time. It looks like the combination was deadly for him."

The officer replied, "It looks to me like he had a massive heart attack, grabbed for the curtains in order to pull himself up and they came out of the wall. I called the coroner and he's on his way. He'll make the determination whether we investigate further, but I'm sure he will do an autopsy."

By this time it was getting close to the start of the Advent service at church. I checked with Mary to see how she was doing with Frieda. Willy had been called and he was on his way from Denver. I spoke some words of comfort to Frieda and told her that I must go to church for the worship service. That was fine with her as long as her son was coming. Mary volunteered to stay with her. I felt uncomfortable leaving her behind while I went to church, but the officers said they would be there a while and I hoped that Willy would get there before they left. All the time that we were there two German Rottweilers had been barking off and on in one of the bedrooms where they were banging against the door. I knew the dogs weren't friendly to strangers. Mary wasn't comfortable around big dogs and Frieda wanted to let them out. When she brought up the suggestion both officers said, "No way! Let them bark." It was obvious they didn't want a confrontation with two angry Rottweilers.

I rushed to church to lead the worship, but my mind was on Mary and the situation at the Holms' not on the worship service. As soon as it was over I rushed back to the house. The coroner had removed the body and the police had left. Willy had not arrived, but Mary was anxious to leave. She told me that she had to keep Frieda occupied in the kitchen while the body was being removed. Also, the neighbor lady, who suggested Frieda call someone, had come to the door in her bare feet and carrying a six-week old baby. Keep in mind that this was about 7:30 in the evening in December. She was concerned about Frieda and wanted to know if there was anything she could do. The dogs were still barking and carrying on.

Willy arrived shortly after I returned to the house. I made sure he was completely filled in on what happened and Mary and I left for home.

The funeral arrangements were set for 2 P.M. on Monday at church. It was to be a memorial service since the body had been cremated. The organist was playing pre-service music while I was making last-minute preparations. I kept my ear attentive to the sound of the door opening in expectation of the arrival of Frieda and Willy. But there was nothing. About five minutes before the service, I peered into the church and was disappointed to see only six people sitting in the church. Mary was there, Maria the wife of my predecessor, two members and a man and his daughter whom I didn't recognize.

I waited for the appointed hour for the funeral and still there was no family. I waited another five minutes while the organist played. When there was still no Frieda and Willy, I called their house. Willy answered the phone, "Hello!"

"Willy, are you coming? We're waiting for you."

"I'm sorry, Pastor. When I got here from Denver Mom was still in her bathrobe. She isn't feeling well. I'm afraid we won't make it to the service."

"What! That's most unusual to have a memorial service with out any family present. Are you absolutely sure that your mother is too sick to make it?"

"Yes! She's dizzy and can barely stand up. She hasn't eaten today and her hair is a mess. I'm afraid it isn't possible."

"I'm sorry your mother isn't feeling well enough to come. I'll see what I can do and I'll get back with you."

"Thanks for being so understanding, Pastor. I'll be staying with Mom for a few days so you can reach me here."

Many thoughts whizzed through my head. *How do I have a service without a family? Do I go ahead with so few people? The poor organist must be getting tired of playing! I've got to make a decision. What do I do?*

As I rounded the corner of the center aisle and saw the few solitary people and that no latecomers arrived, I made my decision. *I will announce that Frieda is too sick to attend the service and that it will be postponed until further notice.*

The organist was relieved to stop playing when he saw me approaching the front of the church. I made my surprising announcement with little additional explanation. Actually, I had none.

The organist packed up his music and the people left. Mary's eyes searched for further explanation, but I had none for her either. She left for home.

I went to my office and returned a couple of phone calls that came in during "the funeral that never happened", opened some mail and tried to do some work. I couldn't accomplish anything. My mind kept returning to Frieda and Willy wondering what they were going through. Finally I decided to go to their home.

When I arrived, there were a couple of cars parked in front of the house. Willy answered the doorbell. "Come in, Pastor. Glad you came over. A few friends stopped by after the service."

I wondered, *what service?* I stepped into the house and saw four of the six people who were at the church. By this time, Frieda was dressed, her hair was combed and she was felling better. The visitors were comforting her in hushed tones. I stepped to where she was sitting and knelt on the floor in front of her. "Frieda, I'm very sorry that you weren't feeling well enough to come to the funeral. I know how much that must have hurt you. I'm happy that you are feeling better now. I came to the house to assure you of God's promise that your Phil is in heaven with his Savior. For Jesus promises, 'I am the resurrection and the life. He who believes in me will live, even though he dies; and whoever lives and believes in me will never die.' (John 11: 25-26)

Someone had compassion on me and brought a chair for me to sit on. I continued to share with Frieda the assurance of Christ's promise that, when we believe in him as our Savior from sin and trust that his suffering and death on the cross was for us, we will live with him in heaven forever. I flowed naturally into the message that I intended to give at the church. When I was finished, I prayed a prayer of comfort and assurance and ended with the benediction.

Frieda was visibly touched and tears welled in her eyes. "Thank you, Pastor," and she squeezed my hands. Willy also thanked me for the comforting words as those gathered in the house nodded their heads in silent agreement. We all visited for a while and when I got up to leave, Willy said to me, "I'm sorry that Mom didn't feel up to making it to the funeral. Maybe we can do it later."

My thoughts returned to the few in church that afternoon and those who had come to the house. I had shared the comforting promise of victory for Phil with Frieda, Willy and two thirds of those who were at church. They didn't need to hear it again, the organist didn't need to have to come and play some more and Mary and Maria already knew the message of salvation well. I didn't want to risk another "no show" of the family so I said, "You've had it! This was your memorial service for Phil."

When Frieda and Willy agreed that it was all right with them, I breathed a sigh of relief.

Willy moved to Colorado Springs to care for his mother. He fixed up the house and made arrangements to have someone at home while he had to be on the road.

Frieda died recently and went to heaven to be with her beloved husband.

She is perfectly happy now.

Chapter 35 – There Are Moments--

Jesus said, "These things I have spoken unto you that my joy may be in you, and that your joy may be full." St. John 15:11

We all experience those moments when we wonder, if God guides all things, why they happen to us like they do. I believe that God looks down from heaven upon our activities much like a parent watches the antics of a young child. When we do something strange, funny or embarrassing he laughs with a great big belly laugh enjoying the silliness of the crown of his creation. I love the picture of "The Laughing Christ" painted by R. Riddick. In that painting Jesus appears to be watching us enjoying every minute of our fumbling human activities. God does have a sense of humor. He made us didn't he?

I was set up at the reception for my Ordination and Installation at St. John's Lutheran Church. Part of the entertainment—if you could call it that—was that I was to match six couples from the congregation who stood before me in random order. This new minister was to try and figure out who went with whom.

It was a recipe for disaster.

I studied each person and tried to match the couples by age, height and similarity of looks. I was operating under the principle that if you lived with someone long enough you began to look like him or her. Also the couples should be about the same age, right?

I could tell that I wasn't doing very well because each time I matched a couple there were snickers from the audience. *Should I revise my match or leave well enough alone?* I decided not to compound my mistakes any farther and let my matches stand. I was already getting sour looks from some of the women that said, "How dare you match me with him! He's definitely not my type. You should be able to see that!" But I couldn't. The men were no help at all. Their faces were as expressionless as if they were playing poker for big bucks.

Finally I declared that my matches were complete and that was the cue for everyone to burst out laughing. The couples were told by the game leader to realign themselves correctly. As they did, it became obvious that I hadn't gotten one couple right. Many people in that close knit community were related and I had matched some brothers with sisters. Well that made sense because they looked alike, but the ages were way off. I didn't make any "brownie points" where I had matched a much older man with a younger woman. I was in real trouble when I matched a couple that had dated seriously for some time but married someone else. But I totally blew it when I said, "I liked my matches better!" That's when the laughter died and so did I.

I didn't hear the criticism from my matches right away, but it slowly filtered back to me over time. I'm sure the reception attendees prayed that I would be much better at being a pastor than I was at matching couples. I think that my ministry redeemed me.

Also early in my ministry at St. John's Mary and I were invited to the 50th Wedding Anniversary of a faithful and loving couple who were very active in our church. The reception hall of the church was packed with family, fellow church members and friends. Now it was a forgone conclusion that any food eaten at the church that had not been blessed by the pastor had no nutritional value. So a family member asked if I would say a blessing and include a prayer of thanks for 50 years for the married couple.

"Sure, I'd be glad to."

So I prayed the most eloquent and meaningful prayer that would come from my heart, asking God's blessing on the food and praising this wonderful and loving couple that had been so blest by our Lord for 50 years. Very satisfied that the food would be beneficial and the couple would receive God's blessing for many more years, I sat down next to Mary and a member of the family leaned over to me and said, "That was a wonderful prayer Pastor. The only thing I would change was that you got their name wrong."

The following spring some members began to consider my prayers very powerful. The planting season started out unusually dry and good moisture was necessary in that farming community. A member came to me before church started and requested that I pray for rain. The request slipped my mind until the end of the worship service, but before I spoke the benediction, I managed to plug in a short prayer that the Lord would send rain. As I turned around with my fingers poised for the blessing, thunder shook the church and immediately rain began to fall. As I looked out over the congregation I could see a good number of the members of the congregation who were wide eyed at God's immediate response to prayer. But it was only a short prayer and the rain ended by the time the members left the church.

The following Sunday I remembered to include a longer petition for rain. It began to rain on Monday and rained steady for two weeks. A member blamed me for the fields being so wet that they couldn't get into them to plant. He asked me to pray that the rain would stop. So, on the following Sunday I prayed for the rain to stop. Obediently the rain stopped on Monday. After that there were a number of believers in my power of prayer. I tried to tell them that it was God's power, but they thought he listened to me better.

After that I didn't have to be asked to pray for rain. I had pretty well grasped the concept of when I needed to pray for it and when I didn't.

It was one of those cool, comfortable nights when one could sleep forever. But it was not to be for me. The phone rang around 3 A.M. and, as I groggily put the receiver to my ear, the anxious voice of Marta Craig's daughter explained, "The nurse at the hospital just called to tell me that Mom has taken a turn for the worse and may only have a few hours to live. Would you please go and visit her?" I interpreted this request to mean that I should go to the hospital immediately. After all, her mom only had a few hours left to live and who knew how long that might be? I pulled myself out of bed, dressed and headed the 20 miles to the hospital in Aberdeen. As I drove I mulled over in my mind how I might minister to the family and what words of comfort I could share with them.

When I arrived at the hospital I was totally shocked to find that there was no family gathered in the room. The room was empty except for Marta who was lying in the bed in a deep coma. Her chest was heaving labored breaths with her mouth open and the distinctive sound of a death rattle was coming from her swollen throat. It was obvious that the nurse was accurate in her diagnosis that she was not going to last much longer. Since hearing is the last sense to go, I read her some comforting passages from Holy Scripture, prayed a prayer of comfort and blessed her with the benediction. I waited a while for any family to appear, but the sun was coming up and no one showed. So I reported to the nurse that I had been there and went home around 6 A.M.

Marta's daughter hadn't explained to me that her plan was to meet some family at the airport that morning and then drive to the hospital. About nine in the morning the family arrived at the hospital and gathered around Marta's bed. They spoke in hushed tones and prayed together.

Even though Marta was in a deep coma she must have heard the familiar voices of her family. With all the strength of a mother's will she decided since her family was there, she wasn't ready to leave them and miss out on sharing in the festivities. With a start she sat up in her bed and exclaimed, "Why are you all looking so sad?" Her family couldn't believe their eyes and drew back at first in shock.

Then they gathered their wits and enjoyed a wonderful visit with their mother who was very much alive.

Marta went home from the hospital a few days later and she lived another three years. The doctors were baffled and the only answer they could come up with for her amazing recovery was that she willed herself to live so that she wouldn't miss the chance of being with her family.

I know that it was another of God's miracles.

A pet peeve of many pastors is the parishioner who falls asleep during the sermon. I'm not sure if we are more offended for the sake of God's Word or for our own self-esteem, but we can see everything from our pulpit perch above the congregation. Olaf Riesner was one of those perennial sleepers.

Olaf would come to church early to assure that he would get a seat on the end of the pew where he could snuggle more comfortably. It didn't bother him that worshipers coming down the middle aisle would have to climb over him to get a seat. Olaf stuck to that end spot like glue. It irked me to watch him. Every time I finished reading the sermon text, Olaf would sit down and wiggle his body until he found his most comfortable position, close his eyes and drop his chin to his chest. Before I was finished with the words "Grace to you and peace from God our Father---" he was asleep. It bothered me that he was so brazen about sleeping in church that he didn't care that I could see him, and he made no pretense that that was the reason he came to church—to get a little extra shut eye.

I took it as long as I could. I had to come up with a solution. Maybe God had a good way to stop him from sleeping, so I took my problem to my Lord in prayer. He heard me and answered me by saying, "What you pray for is good. I'll help you solve your problem." And he provided the way!

The South Dakota District Convention was coming up in January and our church needed to send a delegate. I campaigned for Olaf and he was elected over his objection. I figured that if I could keep him awake for the three days of the convention anything was possible.

I made sure that Olaf sat beside me every minute of that convention. Whenever his head would start to slump I would give him an elbow to his ribs and say, "Pay attention! This is important for you to know because we will be voting on it soon." The first day was torture. I must have elbowed Olaf at least twenty times an hour. My elbow was getting tired not to mention Olaf's ribs. When I would give him a shot with my elbow his head would pop up, his eyes fluttered open and he would emit a grunt—"Huh!"

The second day of the convention saw some improvement. I only needed to elbow Olaf about ten times an hour. The third day was a marked change. Olaf was now anticipating my elbow and his head would bounce up automatically when it would start to sag. The test would come that Sunday.

I watched Olaf as he came into church and found his same comfortable pew. I watched him as I finished reading the sermon text and he sat down, as usual, snuggling himself into the corner of the pew, his eyes went shut and his chin fell to his chest.

At that moment I thought the experiment at the district convention was a miserable failure. I continued preaching, but as soon as Olaf heard my voice his head bobbed up his eyes flashed open and he looked at me with a glassy stare that said, "Now I understand what you were doing to me at the convention."

Well it worked! Thank you Lord.

A few Sundays later I caught another worshiper sleeping. Now to his credit, it was a warm sunny summer day and he had been working long days in the fields. Alfred didn't usually sleep in church but I was determined that I wasn't going to let him fall into an Olaf habit.

Once again the Lord's hand was upon me. I happened to be preaching about how Jesus died for each of us and gave his life on the cross. It struck me, while I was preaching, that I could drive the point home if I called some names of worshipers and told them "Jesus Christ died for you!" I might even kill two birds with one stone if I called out Alfred's name. It seemed like a good plan so I tried it.

"Jesus Christ died for you Julie and for you Darlys and for you Ray! And he also died for you Alfred!" Alfred's eyes flew open, his head shot up and he was about to jump to his feet when his wife grabbed him by the sleeve pulling him back down. He blinked his eyes at me a couple of times as if to ask, "Why did you call my name?" I'm sure his wife filled him in after the worship service because Alfred never slept in church again. At least not while I was preaching.

On a sunny day in late October there was a beautiful covering of fresh snow on the ground and I was driving to Peace Church to attend a ladies meeting at one of the homes. I was dressed all in black, which was standard attire for the well-dressed clergy at the time. It was goose season and as I came to the crest of a hill I could see a large flock of geese was feeding in a field up ahead. During hunting season I always carried my shotgun in the trunk of the car in case such an opportunity arose. A glance at my wristwatch told me that I had a few extra minutes to spare before the ladies meeting, so I pulled off the road and retrieved my gun from the trunk. I carefully squeezed through the fence and began trudging through the snow toward the flock of geese. The crest of the hill ahead hid my approach from the geese, but I was painfully aware that my feet were getting wet and that I made a stark figure in my black coat against the white snow. But no worry I had the element of surprise over the geese. That was until I reached about ten feet from the top of the hill and stuck my head up to see where the geese were. That was where I went wrong. The geese were just 50 feet away but I wanted to take a few more steps up the hill to get a better shot. I ducked down hoping the geese hadn't spotted me but it was too late. The watch goose had spotted me and gave the warning signal to the other birds. From my crouched position I heard the tremendous sound of honking and flapping wings. I rose from my crouch to attack the flock but, as I peeked over the top of the hill, the geese had taken off in the opposite direction and were already out of shotgun range.

I didn't even get one shot!

Dejectedly I made my way back to the car realizing that people driving by must have been wondering what in the world this nattily attired pastor was doing hiking out on a snow covered field with a shotgun in his arm. Maybe they figured it out when they saw the flock flying away, because only one church member asked what I was doing. I told him "I was chasing geese." It was the truth because I certainly wasn't hunting, bird watching maybe. That seemed to satisfy him because he didn't question me anymore.

I drove on to the meeting believing that my embarrassment was behind me, but I was wrong. The ladies and I sat in a circle around the living room and visited until the time for the meeting to start. The appointed time arrived and the chairlady called the meeting to order. It was then that I decided to investigate the reason for an unusual draft that was focusing on my lap. Oh no, I forgot to zip up my pants! Thinking quickly I implored, "Let's bow our heads and begin our meeting with a prayer." This was standard procedure anyway, so all of the ladies dutifully bowed their heads for prayer. I glanced around to make sure all heads were bowed and when I was satisfied, I zipped up my pants. I think I pulled it off because there was not even a smile when all heads were raised following the prayer. It was either that or the ladies had great control.

During the time that I served St. John's Lutheran Church in Groton, South Dakota I enjoyed the people and found it to be an interesting experience. I recall the first Sunday that I preached. Evidently the congregation was not used to a preacher with a strong voice. Maybe it was a combination of my starting the sermon forcefully and the P. A. system being turned up too loud, but my voice bellowed into the congregation. I noticed many worshipers get wide-eyed and a few turned down their hearing aids. The members got used to my voice after a few Sundays and so did the P.A. operator.

One Sunday after the worship service, I went into the pastor's office to take off my robe. I was surprised to see that the congregation's treasurer was alone in the room counting the offering. I asked him if this was the usual practice and he answered, "Yes." I considered how I might approach this diplomatically and decided the direct approach was best. "Did you ever stop to realize that there is a danger of impropriety when the same person who counts the offering and deposits it in the bank is the same person who writes the checks?"

"No, I never gave it any thought," he said reflectively.

"You may be as honest as the day is long, but the next person to hold your job might not be. At the next church council meeting I'm going to request that a committee of counters be set up so that more than one person is responsible for counting and depositing the offering. This will also protect you from any criticism."

"That's a great idea Pastor, I was getting tired of doing it all myself anyway."

I was relieved to hear that he wasn't offended by my suggestion and that he supported the idea. The council gave approval of having a committee of counters and everything worked very well after that.

When Christmas time rolled around, the congregation had a unique way of solving the problem of limited space for the Christmas tree. There was no room in the sanctuary because the communion rails extended from one wall to the other. There was a small space next to the pulpit that was ideal for the tree's placement, but the congregation liked a tree that stood about 18 feet. This size tree left no room for anyone coming down the side aisle to get to the front of the church for communion. Their solution was to tie the top of the tree with a rope and suspend it from the ceiling. I thought that was ingenious.

As the Christmas season progressed, I discovered there was an inherent problem with their solution. I wondered, at first, why the first row on the pulpit side was vacant. It became obvious when the first person passed by the tree and gave it a shove, the trunk swung back like a pendulum over the first row of pews. New members or visitors, who were unaware of the danger of the swinging Christmas tree, would sit in that row and have to duck as the trunk swung over their heads. Seasoned members knew better than to sit in that location during Christmas.

During the time of my ministry at the church in Groton, a new parsonage was being built. The story concocted by some members was that the previous pastor wanted a new parsonage and when the congregation said, "No!" He burned it down. Well that wasn't quite accurate.

I had been in that parsonage and it was old and pretty ramshakled. The heating system was antiquated as were most appliances in the house. As an example, the coat hangers by the backdoor were large nails pounded into the wall. Instead of building, the congregation was interested in purchasing a nearby home that was in better shape but still old. But as most congregational decisions ruminate, there was no rush.

Still no decision on a parsonage had been made by the time spring came and the pastor was considering a call to a parish in another state. There had been some warm days and the pastor had turned off the furnace. But as the time for their Vacation Bible School arrived, a cold spell hit. The pastor lit the furnace and, fortunately, he and his family went to the church for VBS. The furnace malfunctioned while they were gone and started a fire. It was confined to the basement and was extinguished quickly, but it left extensive smoke damage to the house and its contents including the pastoral family goods.

All things considered, the pastor saw some great challenges in the call and decided to accept it. It was an opportunity for him to advance his ministry and to move his family out of a smoky house.

Before the family moved, adding insult to injury, the congregation decided that since the house was unlivable they would tear it down and build a new one on the same location. Some members of the congregation voiced their thought *that serves him right for burning our parsonage down and then accepting a call on top of it.* Right or wrong, there is no way to control what people will think.

The new parsonage was completed in my tenure at St. John's. It was a beautiful new split-foyer home built by a member who was a contractor. He used many members for sweat equity and the result was that the congregation had a brand new parsonage for a fraction of the normal cost to build it. The pastor and his family who accepted the call in the fall loved the new parsonage.

Sometimes it is your children that embarrass you. Normally our children were well behaved in church and, to make sure they paid attention, Mary moved up to the third row for the first time. Our son's second birthday fell on Sunday that year and he was pretty keyed up. He just couldn't sit still. Mary tried to keep him on her lap but that didn't work. While I was preaching I observed his wiggling and rejection of his mother's attempts to make him sit still as long as I could. Finally I couldn't hold back any longer. I called his name "Scott!" He didn't hear me so I called it a little louder "Scott!" Again there was no response from him so I raised my voice directly into the microphone, "**Scott**!" This time Scott heard me and reacted with a startled jump and simultaneously two boys named Scott also jumped in the back of the church. One boy was a visitor.

After the worship service I explained to the parents why I had called their sons' names from the pulpit and they both replied that it probably did them good too.

Some years later when we lived in Rapid City we were gathered for worship when a lady heavily dowsed with perfume entered the pew and sat down next to Scott. In all the innocence of a four-year-old he called it as he saw it. He said to his mother in a voice that echoed through the congregation, "She stinks!"

There were a few titters in the congregation and although the lady never said a word, I carried the guilt for my son's comment for almost 25 years. The perfumed lady and her husband were in Colorado Springs not long ago and they stopped to visit us. I figured that she couldn't be too upset since she wanted to see us. I wondered if time had been a healer or if she came for an apology. After we had visited for a while, I delicately brought up the subject of Scott's comment. "Oh that's what he said! I heard him say something but I didn't understand him." Now I was sorry that I brought it up but she was very understanding because she had children of her own.

Why had I carried that guilt for all those years?

On another occasion in Colorado Springs I was at home on a Friday night and a ferocious blizzard was raging outside. The snow was piling up by the feet and the wind was blowing it into great drifts. Even four-wheel drive vehicles were having great difficulty getting around. The TV weatherman was warning everyone to stay home and off the streets. I was just thinking how happy I was to be home with no reason to go out into the cold and snow when the telephone rang. It was Walter who lived alone near the church, which was about eight miles away from where we lived.

He pleaded, "Pastor, I think I'm having a heart attack. I need help. I don't know anyone else to call. Could you come and drive me to the hospital?"

"What makes you think you are having a heart attack?'

"I don't feel so good and there is a pain going down my left arm."

"Walter, if you don't know, there is a blizzard going on outside and I'm sure that I can't make it to you house. I'll try to think of some way to get you to the hospital and I'll call you back."

"I'm sorry to bother you Pastor, I know there is a blizzard going on but I didn't know where else to turn."

"I call you right back."

After I hung up I considered if there were any members that lived close to Walter with a four-wheel drive vehicle but I couldn't come up with any. I explained the situation to Mary and she tried to think of a solution to the problem. The only option we could come up with was to call 911. I called Walter back to let him know what my only option was, but he didn't answer his phone.

Now I had visions of Walter lying on the floor clutching his chest with a severe heart attack and I had to act fast. So I dialed 911, gave them Walter's name and address and explained his problem.

A few days later after the blizzard subsided, Walter called me. "Pastor, why did you send the paramedics to my home the other night without telling me you were going to do that?"

"Well Walter," I explained, "I tried to call you back but you never answered the phone and I thought you might be in need of emergency medical treatment. There was no way I could get to you and no one else I dared send out in the storm, so I did what I thought was best and dialed 911."

"Oh Pastor, I wasn't suffering a heart attack! I was just feeling lonely and wanted someone to come and visit me and you sent the paramedics. It's going to cost me around $300.00 for that call."

"I'm sorry that it's going to cost you some money but you cried "wolf" on a night that wasn't fit for anyone to be out on the streets. If it had been decent weather I would have been there for you, but as it was, you only thought of your loneliness and gave no consideration for the safety of someone else. The $300.00 is the price you must pay for a lesson on consideration for others."

Walter learned his lesson and never called me for fake assistance again.

One afternoon, while I was working on my sermon, the telephone rang and I was asked to make a hospital call on a man who had surgery at St. Francis Hospital. It was a beautiful day and I could use the exercise so I walked the short distance since the hospital was across the street. I located Harley's room and knocked as I entered. Harley reminded me of Bob Hope. He looked like Bob Hope and loved to tell jokes just like the old master of comedy. Harley had just returned to his room from the recovery unit following surgery on his stomach and upper intestines. He was still pretty groggy from the anesthetic, but he was in good spirits as he talked about his surgery.

He told me that this was the second time they had to do it. After the first surgery the nurse brought him some liquid to drink and as he poured it into his mouth he sprouted a leak at the incision in his stomach. The surgeon had nicked his stomach by accident. He was good-natured about it and there was no hint of a lawsuit in his horizon. But he thought it hilarious that he received two operations for the price of one.

Two days after Harley's release from the hospital, he called me and said that if I wanted a good laugh I should come over to the house. I thought it would be a good idea to do a follow-up visit on him anyway, so I went plus I could also use a good laugh.

When I arrived, Harley was sitting at his kitchen nook with a sheepish grin on his face. He greeted me with a hearty, "Hello Pastor G! Guess where I was during the night?" Well, in his recovering condition I knew he couldn't have gone too far, but I didn't guess. "They took me back to the hospital in an ambulance!" he chortled.

"Now what went wrong?"

"Well pastor, it was all my fault. I couldn't get to sleep last night. I lay in bed for hours and tried everything I knew to try and get to sleep but nothing worked. I even tried counting sheep. Finally in total frustration I got up and came into the kitchen. I wasn't supposed to have any solid food yet, but I could have liquids. The thought of a drink came to my mind and my mouth watered. I thought it might relax me so I could fall asleep. So I mixed myself a highball and sat down here at the table. I drank about half of my drink when "wham" it reacted with my pain medication. I didn't know what hit me. I must have passed out or something, but when I came to enough to realize that I was in trouble, I managed to reach the phone behind me and dialed 911. The voice that answered the call asked what was the nature of my emergency. I told her that I wasn't sure what my problem was but all I knew is that I felt dizzy and had leaky feet." She said, "you have what?" I said, "I have leaky feet!"

"I'll get an ambulance over there right away but you stay on the phone and talk to me until it arrives.'"

"I'm sure she thought I was nuts. There was quite a commotion in the neighborhood when the ambulance and fire truck arrived with their sirens blaring at 2 A.M. The paramedics checked me out and I was still quite confused so they loaded me into the ambulance and took me the five blocks to the hospital. By the time I got there my mind cleared enough to realize what had happened. When that drink hit me and I passed out, the plastic glass must have slid out of my hand onto the floor. The cold liquid and ice cubes hit my feet and brought me too enough to dial 911. I'm sure the girl on the phone thought she had a real weirdo on the line but, as I recall, she was very nice. There was not much they could do for me in the emergency room but let the effects of the alcohol wear off and that didn't take too long. Then they sent me home. So I didn't get much sleep last night."

We laughed together about him having "leaky feet" but I decided not to offer him Holy Communion just in case he was still on pain medication.

A friend who was a funeral director called me and shared a sad story about a young couple with a one-year-old son who was traveling through the area. The boy suddenly became ill and by the time they got him to the hospital he was unconscious. He died within hours. The couple was grieving over the loss of their only child. The hospital personnel helped them contact a funeral director. My friend wanted me to have the service. I told him that I would help in any way I could.

Because the couple was in the process of moving from one coast to another, they wanted to have the service as soon as possible. I met them early that afternoon so that I could get acquainted and determine what comforting ministry they needed. They had a strong trust in Jesus as their Savior, which made my ministry to them much easier. We visited awhile and I felt a kinship with them because we were about the same age. The three of us held hands and we prayed together for God's strength and comfort.

The funeral director came into the room and said that their son was ready for viewing. The mother tensed noticeably. I ushered the couple into the chapel for their first glimpse of their son since they left him lying on the hospital bed. I was not prepared for the sight of that little boy in the tiny casket. It was completely open from head to toe revealing a beautiful little boy with a perfect complexion and blonde hair, which was carefully combed. He wore khaki pants with a plaid shirt and a little sweater vest. For some reason what hit my heart hard were the tiny tennis shoes on his feet. I thought about my children, who were similar in age, and how much it would hurt if I had to leave one of them behind in an unfamiliar place. It would be unbearable.

I knew it was for this young couple too. The mother kept holding on to those little tennis shoes and she didn't want to let go. She and the father wept openly and I tried to choke back my own tears with little success. This was going to be a tough funeral for me to get through.

The service followed with only the couple, the funeral director and myself so we stood next to the little casket. The mother leaned against it to steady herself and kept hold of the tiny shoes. It was very personal. I tried to comfort the parents, as much as possible, with scriptural examples of Jesus' love for little children and his promises that the kingdom of heaven belongs to them. I tried to make the picture of Jesus blessing the little children in St. Luke 18: 15-17, as visual to them as I could. I wanted them to picture their son with a big smile on his face sitting on Jesus' lap in heaven receiving his blessing. I wanted them to be comforted with the reassurance that their son was in the loving arms of his Lord and that he was happy and would be cared for by his Savior forever. I wanted them to know that they would see their son again when they were called to their heavenly rest.

My words--no, God's words--seemed to take hold and comfort them for they stopped crying and the mother let go of the tiny shoes. The casket was closed and we followed it to the cemetery where it was placed in the ground. My last words were to reassure the couple that the body of their son that we were putting into the ground was only the temporary shell that he occupied on this earth. That he would be given a new resurrected body in heaven. "Keep looking up" I told them, "for that's where your son is now. That's our goal. He has received his victory earlier than most, but victory none-the-less. God was gracious to your son and he will also comfort you."

"Thank you!" they said with tears in their eyes.

I hugged them both and they drove away. The mother looked out the car's back window until she could no longer see her son's grave. I waved goodbye and she smiled at me and waved back as their car disappeared around the corner.

Epilogue

Following my retirement from full-time ministry in 2002, Mary and I took a two-month RV tour of the southern states and then visited family and friends in Illinois, Iowa, Minnesota and South Dakota. I still preach on occasion, make homebound communion visits on members of Immanuel and visit in the hospitals.

I have recently joined the Colorado Springs Police Department as a chaplain. I serve on call for two days a month and drive a car marked, "Chaplain- Colorado Springs Police Department." It has a police radio, flashing lights but no siren. I don't carry a gun but there is a protective vest for me to wear. Chaplains also do ride-a-longs with police officers, which I find interesting and rewarding. In the short time that I have been a chaplain I have been involved in some very interesting situations. If I write another book it could be about my experiences as a police chaplain.

Time will tell.

About the author

With more than 40 years experience in a ministry where God was his constant guide and support, Timothy Grassinger realized that his stories could be a source of spiritual growth to the lives of others. He served a total of four parishes during his ministry and each one had its own unique character and experience.

He was born at St. Paul, Minnesota in 1940 during World War II. He attended Concordia Theological Seminary of The Lutheran Church-Missouri Synod in Springfield, Illinois graduating in 1965. His first call was to a dual parish in eastern South Dakota at Columbia and rural Hecla. From there he and his growing family moved to Rapid City at the opposite end of the state in 1971. After six years of ministry there, the family moved to Colorado Springs, where he served Immanuel Lutheran Church for 25 years until his retirement.

Pastor Grassinger enjoyed a variety of ministry experiences most of which where ordinary and others that were unusual and tested his faith. The character of his ministry was that he always desired to serve his flock in the example of Christ and to love them no matter what.

Printed in the United States
By Bookmasters